*To the young women of Girlguiding, for all your adventures yet to come –* A. M.

*For Vivienne Jackson, who filled my childhood with adventures –* C. R.

First published 2020 by Walker Books Ltd
87 Vauxhall Walk, London SE11 5HJ

2 4 6 8 10 9 7 5 3 1

Text © 2020 Anna McNuff
Illustrations © 2020 Clair Rossiter

The right of Anna McNuff and Clair Rossiter to be identified as author and illustrator respectively of this work has been asserted by them in accordance with the Copyright, Designs and Patents Act 1988

This book has been typeset in Intro Regular

Printed in China

British Library Cataloguing in Publication Data:
a catalogue record for this book is available from the British Library

ISBN 978-1-4063-8863-3

www.walker.co.uk

# THIS BOOK BELONGS TO

. . . . . . . . . . . . . . . . . . . . . . . . . . . . . . . . . . . . . . . . . . . . . . . . .

## WARNING

### Adult supervision required.

This book contains a number
of dangerous activities that
should be carried out under
the supervision of an adult.

Not suitable for children
under seven years.

Anna McNuff

# 100 Adventures to Have Before You Grow Up

Illustrated
By
CLAIR ROSSITER

WALKER BOOKS
AND SUBSIDIARIES
LONDON • BOSTON • SYDNEY • AUCKLAND

# CONTENTS

Hello, my fellow adventurer,

Once upon a time I decided to cycle across the Great Basin Desert in the USA. Before I left a tiny town on the outskirts of the desert, I felt nervous about what I was going to find. This was a place I'd never been to before and a landscape full of unknowns. Anything could happen. I began my journey, cycling up steep mountain passes and whizzing across dusty plateaus. Often there was no other sound apart from the whirr of my wheels and my breath as I puffed and pedalled.

In the end, hidden among the scrub of the desert and covered by a blanket of twinkling stars, I found exactly what I was looking for: adventure.

Since that time in the desert, I've filled my life with as many adventures as possible. I've cycled, hiked, rollerbladed, swum and run (sometimes in fancy dress, sometimes in bare feet) over 20,000 miles across the planet. On my adventures, I've discovered that our world is an amazing place, and that, better still, you don't even have to travel far to experience its wonder. Adventures can be found everywhere: in the nearby woods, at your local park and even in your nanna's back garden.

When I think about how many new places there are in the world to explore, I feel like my brain is going to explode. I've spent years adventuring and I've barely scratched the surface! How can I sit still at home when there are mountains to climb, rivers to raft down, forests to run through and ancient ruins to explore? There are hundreds – no, thousands – of adventures you can have in a lifetime.

I didn't think you could fit a book of a thousand adventures on your bookshelf, so I've given myself the difficult job of choosing just a hundred of the most awesome adventures that I think everyone should try. I've chosen ones that begin on your doorstep and ones that take you further afield. There are adventures you can do with your friends, with your family and some where you can go it alone.

Big or small, near or far, one thing's for certain: an adventure won't just drop into your lap one day while you're sitting inside in your pyjamas. You must seek out adventure. You have to be brave and dare to go out into the unknown like the intrepid explorers of the past and the bold adventurers of today. You must be prepared to try new things, take a few deep breaths and scare yourself silly. You must fly by the seat of your adventure pants, because the feeling you get from pushing yourself to a new limit is like nothing else.

Now stop reading this, pick one of these adventures and get outdoors! There are dens to build, trees to climb and sledges to make. There are waves to surf, trails to run and wild animals to spot.

It's all out there waiting for you.

Happy adventuring!

Anna

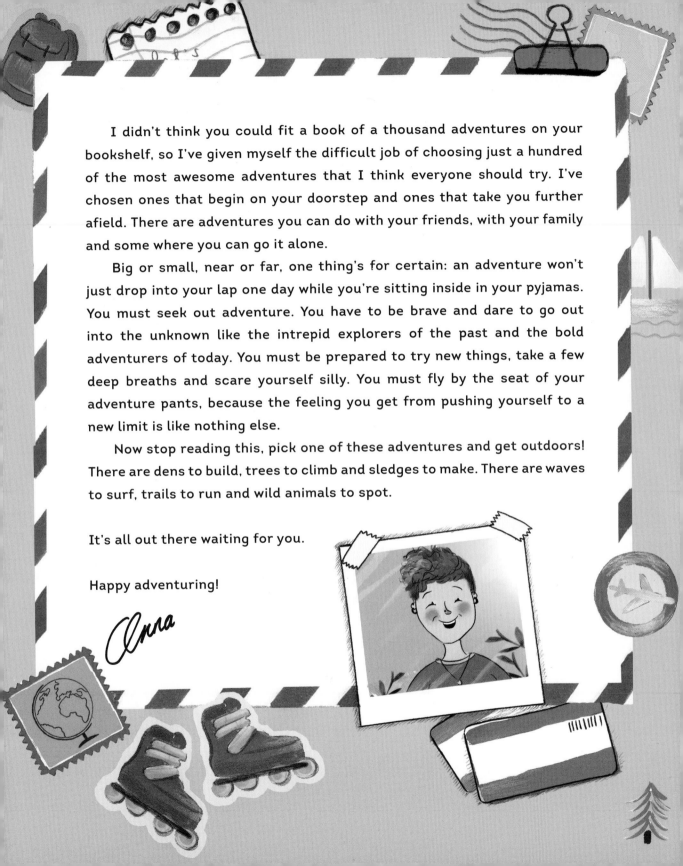

# USING THIS BOOK

As you take on the adventures in this book, use these handy guides to help you with your planning.

## AROUND THE WORLD
Incredible adventure destinations

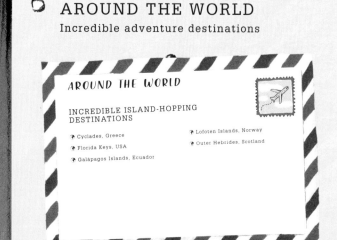

### AROUND THE WORLD

**INCREDIBLE ISLAND-HOPPING DESTINATIONS**

- Cyclades, Greece
- Florida Keys, USA
- Galápagos Islands, Ecuador
- Lofoten Islands, Norway
- Outer Hebrides, Scotland

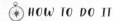

## HOW TO DO IT
Step-by-step guides to the adventures

### ✦ HOW TO DO IT

1. Find an expert who knows the area and the best route to take.

2. Choose your footwear carefully – trainers or boots with good grip are essential.

3. When you're scrambling, look for less-steep sections of rock with ledges for your feet. Look for rocks that you can wrap your fingers around and use as handholds. Often the best routes reveal themselves as you go along.

4. Once you've finished a section, make sure you take a good look at what you just shimmied your way across, and stop to shout "WOWSERS!"

5. Remember that what goes up must come down. Save some energy and jelly beans for the scramble down.

## ADVENTURE INSPIRATION
Helpful ideas for planning your adventure

### 📝 ADVENTURE INSPIRATION

**DECIDE YOUR DISTANCE**
How far do you want to run each day? If you're new to running, up to 10 kilometres per day will allow for some great exploring.

**CHOOSE YOUR ROUTE**
Think about what kind of scenery you want to run through. Would you like to explore historic sites like old castles? Or perhaps you'd prefer to see a lake or river? How about running alongside waves crashing into a rugged coastline? Tailor the route to what you want to see because the more you love the scenery, the more it'll spur you on. National trails make great routes and often have maps available online.

**PLAN YOUR SUPPLIES**
If there are lots of little towns en route, then you won't need to carry much food or water, but if you're heading into the wilderness, pack some sandwiches.

**FIND A PLACE TO SLEEP**
Are you going to stay in a tent or a hostel? If you opt for a tent you can get an adult to carry it and other essentials.

## WHEN YOU GROW UP
Inspirational accounts of real-life adventurers

### WHEN YOU GROW UP
Vonetta Flowers dreamed of becoming an Olympian. When she failed to make the track-and-field team, she turned to bobsledding. Two years later, she and her teammate made history by winning gold at the first Olympic bobsled event for women.

**Don't forget to update the checklist on p.140-41 after every adventure! Can you tick off all 100 of them?**

# ADVENTURE SAFELY

Adventures are meant to push you to new limits and take you out of your comfort zone. That means that they can also be dangerous, so it is important you take care of yourself. Never go adventuring without a responsible and experienced adult to supervise you.

When you are outdoors, respect your environment. Always check the weather before you set off. Water can be deep, cold and fast-moving. Never enter the water by yourself and always wear appropriate safety equipment, such as a buoyancy aid and wetsuit. The ground can be wet, slippery and rocky, so wear sensible footwear and stick to marked paths where possible. Wear a helmet if you are cycling, climbing or tackling snowsports or watersports. Stay aware of potential hazards around you, such as cars or farm animals.

# ADVENTURE RESPONSIBLY

Adventures take you out into some of the most beautiful, remote and extreme places in the world. Make sure you have permission to be in that place and remember to close any gates behind you and obey signs and warnings. You have a responsibility to take care of the sites you visit so that future adventurers can enjoy them too. Where possible, try to reuse and recycle any items needed for an adventure. When there, always leave the area exactly how you found it. Take away your litter, don't disturb any wildlife and forage responsibly with a trained adult.

# PACKING LIST

Adventures are always better with the right kit. No one wants to get soggy socks halfway through an adventure and then wish they had a spare pair! Here are some trusty adventure essentials that will never let you down:

- [ ] Day rucksack
- [ ] Gloves
- [ ] Hat (either a cap or woolly one)
- [ ] Hiking boots
- [ ] Safety gear (such as a buoyancy aid or helmet)
- [ ] Sleeping bag
- [ ] Sleeping mat
- [ ] Snacks
- [ ] Spare socks
- [ ] Sun cream
- [ ] Swimwear
- [ ] Thermal base layers
- [ ] Torch
- [ ] Trainers
- [ ] Water bottle
- [ ] Waterproof jacket
- [ ] Waterproof trousers
- [ ] Wetsuit

# 1. CLIMB A MOUNTAIN

Nothing beats the feeling of standing higher than the clouds on the top of a mountain with fresh, clean air whipping your cheeks. It's even more satisfying when you've had to spend hours - or even days - huffing and puffing your way to the mountain's summit.

Climbing a mountain isn't easy and you will need an experienced adult to come with you. The path (if there is a path) is likely to be steep and narrow, parts of the climb might be exposed to the elements and, if you are going high enough, you'll come across snow and slippery ice. But that's exactly what makes the adventure so special - it's a challenge!

## AROUND THE WORLD

### AWE-INSPIRING SUMMITS

- Ben Nevis, UK: 1,345 metres

- Aoraki (Mount Cook), New Zealand: 3,724 metres

- Mont Blanc, France/Italy: 4,808 metres

- Aconcagua, Argentina: 6,962 metres

- Mount Everest, Nepal/China: 8,848 metres

# ADVENTURE INSPIRATION

## PACE YOURSELF

Even if you feel superhuman in the
first hour, you have a long day ahead.
Usually a climb has at least one very
steep section, so always keep a little
bit of energy in the tank.

## TAKE LAYERS

The weather is often changeable on
a mountain so it's important to make
sure you have the right clothing.
It's best to pack lots of thin-but-warm
layers, so that you can make small
adjustments to your body temperature.

## CHOOSE GOOD SNACKS

There's nothing worse than having
an energy lull halfway up a climb
and realizing all you have left is a
squashed, brown banana. Pack your
favourite snack as a treat for when
you need it. Pack some extras too,
just in case!

## WATCH THE DAWN BREAK

Why not spend the night wild camping
just below the summit so you can
be at the top for
sunrise?

### WHEN YOU GROW UP

Junko Tabei was the first
woman to reach the summit
of Mount Everest, the world's
highest mountain. She's also
the first woman to climb all
Seven Summits (the highest
mountains on each of the
seven continents).

# 2. BE A WASTE WARRIOR

Our rubbish doesn't always end up in the right place. Litter that isn't thrown in the bin or recycled travels down rivers and streams and out into the ocean, where it can harm wildlife in many different ways.

With your family and friends, go on an adventure to collect litter before it reaches the sea. Take bin bags, gloves and, if you can find one, a special litter-picking claw. Look for plastic litter, which is especially bad for the environment, like coffee cups, plastic bottles, straws and plastic bags. Avoid picking up broken glass, needles or poo.

Unfortunately you can find litter almost anywhere, so this adventure will lead you to all sorts of strange and marvellous places. And you'll feel awesome at the end, knowing that you've helped to restore the beauty of Planet Earth.

Once you've collected your litter, recycle what you can and bin everything else. And don't forget to wash your hands afterwards!

 ADVENTURE INSPIRATION

## RUN AND PICK
Go for a run and do two laps. On the first lap, look for plastic and litter. On the second, whip out your bin bag and gather as many pieces as you can.

## PADDLE AND PICK
Head off for the afternoon in a canoe or kayak or on a stand-up paddleboard. You'll find lots of pieces of litter trapped in bushes at the side of canals and rivers or on beaches.

## STROLL AND PICK
Go down to your nearest beach and collect all the litter you can see. Just when that piece of plastic threatens to escape into the ocean and harm a bird or animal, you can swoop down and be a hero with a bin bag.

# 3. VISIT THE OLDEST BUILDING NEARBY

Adventures don't all have to be about the present. Going adventuring in the past can be awesome too. Exploring an ancient building is a way of finding out more about the people who once lived there. There might be stories of gruesome battles, hoards of treasure or delicious feasts.

This is a great adventure to do with your friends or family. You can start the research on your own and find one or two buildings nearby that are open to the public and you might like to visit. When researching your area, think about why the building was built and who might have lived there. Once you've decided on the building, set off to greet the kings, queens, kitchen maids and warriors of the past.

## AROUND THE WORLD

### AWESOME ANCIENT BUILDINGS

- The Pyramids of Giza, Egypt; built in 2575–2465 BCE

- Parthenon, Greece; built in mid-5th century BCE

- Mont-Saint-Michel, France; built in 8th century CE

- Canterbury Cathedral, UK; current building constructed in 1070–77

- The Winter Palace, Russia; building began in 1703

# 4. TRAVEL BY SKI

Skiing is one of the most efficient ways to travel through snow. Skis allow you to whizz down hills, move across flats and, if you're feeling really energetic, climb, or "skin", your way up mountains.

If you're new to winter sports, decide what kind of skiing you want to try. Cross-country skiing is when you ski across flat ground. Downhill skiing involves going down the slopes of a mountain as fast as you can. Ski touring is a combination of the two, and means travelling long distances up, down and across mountains and valleys.

If you don't live in a place where it snows often, don't forget your local dry ski-slope or snow dome. Start mastering the basics there with some lessons. Once you've got your ski legs, why not try a point-to-point adventure out in the snow?

## AROUND THE WORLD

### WHERE TO TAKE TO THE TRAILS

- 🌐 Antarctica
- 🌐 Austria
- 🌐 Canada
- 🌐 France
- 🌐 Greenland
- 🌐 Italy
- 🌐 Japan
- 🌐 Norway
- 🌐 Switzerland
- 🌐 USA

## WHEN YOU GROW UP

Felicity Aston was the first woman to ski alone across the continent of Antarctica. She completed a 1,084-mile journey in 59 days, which took her via the South Pole and through temperatures as low as -30°C. She pulled two sledges full of supplies, weighing a total of 85 kilograms, which was more than her own body weight.

## HOW TO DO IT

1. Set aside a day and find a national park with ski trails, or a mountain range where there are ski lifts to connect multiple ski runs.

2. Find a map of the piste. Work with an experienced skier (this could be a parent, family member or instructor) to decide on a route. You could go from A to B and back to A, or try a circuit where you pass through each place once and end up back where you started. Figure out where you can stop for hot drinks and snacks along the way.

3. Ski touring is tiring because you have to push along flat sections, which uses lots of different muscles. To make good progress when "skating" along the flats, think about pushing one side of your body forwards at a time. That means that when your left arm and pole are held out in front of your body, your right foot and ski are behind your body. Keep switching from left to right and you'll find a rhythm.

4. Once you've done some day trips by ski you could take things to the next level and try an overnight trip, staying in a mountain hut or log cabin.

# 5. BUILD A DEN AND SLEEP IN IT

A den is an awesome secret meeting place as well as a useful shelter from the elements. Build your den anywhere with the help of some friends: outside in your garden using branches, or indoors with sofa cushions and cardboard boxes. Make sure you pack everything you need for a night sleeping out in your hideaway: snacks, a torch and a sleeping bag. Don't forget to decide who will be allowed inside your den. Why don't you come up with a top-secret password?

## TOP TIP

If you're using branches, put the narrower ends close to the ground. That way, if they break, the den wall just slips downward as opposed to caving in.

Top secret!

# ADVENTURE INSPIRATION

## CLASSIC DEN

The quickest way to make a sturdy den is to build an A-frame out of fallen tree branches. Use two short branches to create the shape of an "A". This will be the opening to your den. Then use a long branch to reach from the top of the "A" down to the ground. Fill in the gaps with ferns, leaves and smaller branches.

## TREE-BRANCH DEN

Find a tree with a strong horizontal branch that is about 1.5 metres off the ground. Use this branch as your frame and arrange smaller fallen branches along the branch in an "A" shape.

## ROUND DEN

Tie 6–8 long thick branches of equal length together at one end with rope, then hoist them upright and separate out the other ends to form a circular base. Fill in the gaps in the frame with straight branches and leaves.

## INDOOR DEN

Grab whatever you can find in your home – blankets, chairs, cushions, fairy lights, cardboard boxes – and make yourself a cosy hideaway.

# 6. GO FORAGING

Did you know that nature can be a giant supermarket? Of course, the aisles might look a little different from a normal supermarket, and you won't need to pay a thing at the checkout, but there are shelves upon shelves of fresh, nutritious nibbles to be had – if you know what you're looking for.

Whenever you go foraging, you must have a trained adult with you who knows exactly what is safe and tasty to eat, as some plants are poisonous. Always pick responsibly and make sure you leave enough for wildlife and don't damage any habitats.

**TOP TIP**

The best times to forage for food are spring and autumn.

 ## SPOTTER'S GUIDE: FORAGING

## NETTLES

Stinging nettles aren't just annoying nuisances when you're trying to find a lost ball. They are actually very good for you and packed with vitamins and minerals. You'll need gloves to pick them, but then you can pop a few leaves in boiling water and sit back and relax with a cup of nettle tea. You can also wilt them in a saucepan with melted butter, like spinach, or serve them in a soup. Yum!

## WOOD SORREL

Wood sorrel looks a bit like clover so be careful – the two taste very different. Sorrel has a delicious lemony flavour and the sourness works brilliantly with fish, greens or in a salad.

## ELDERFLOWER

Frothy white elderflowers grow in clusters on elder trees in springtime. They smell delicious! Pick them and make homemade elderflower cordial, fritters or jam.

## BLACKBERRIES

Blackberries are the best grab-and-go foraging snack in the late summer and early autumn. Deliciously sweet, they should be deep purple and almost black when they're picked.

# 7. FIND A NATURAL HOT SPRING AND BATHE IN IT

Imagine sinking into a warm and gently bubbling pool. You are surrounded by wild forests or snow-capped mountains. There's not a rubber duck in sight and no one has had to run the hot tap to get the water temperature just right. Nature took care of that when it created the hot spring.

There are thousands of natural hot springs all over the world. They are formed when heat from the Earth's crust escapes into pools of water and makes them warm. Every spring is different due to the temperature and minerals in the water, which are usually a mixture of calcium, sodium, magnesium and iron. Some springs are believed to have healing properties – so kick back, relax and let nature soothe your tired adventure-muscles.

### TOP TIP

Never put your head under the water in a hot spring – tiny toxic organisms can lurk there.

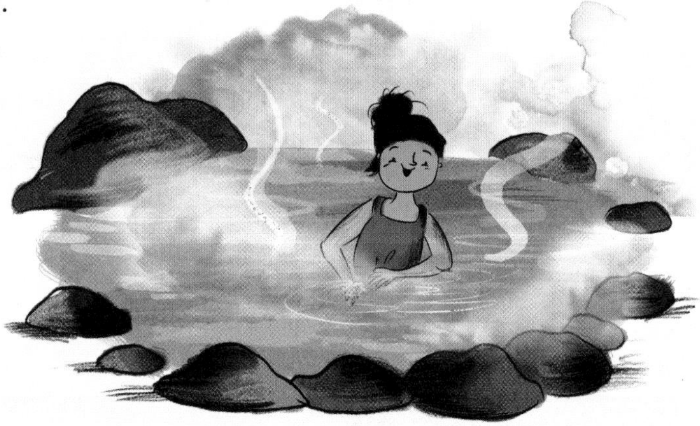

## AROUND THE WORLD

### RELAXING HOT SPRINGS

- Blue Lagoon, Iceland
- Buxton, UK
- Puritama Hot Springs, Chile
- Terme di Saturnia, Italy
- Travertine Hot Springs, USA

# 8. DO A FANCY-DRESS RUN

Life is better in fancy dress! With a little bit of face-paint and a costume, you can transform yourself into a superhero, an animal or a pirate – anything you want! So why not add a bit of fun to your running adventures by dressing up for them? Get your friends involved too.

Not only will the run get your heart pounding and your adrenaline racing, you'll get a real giggle from making your costume. The running becomes the easy part when there's a theme and outfit to be decided. Just don't forget to take photos!

### WHEN YOU GROW UP

Jamie McDonald – who goes by Adventureman – found his inner superhero when he ran 5,000 miles across Canada in fancy dress. However, his powers couldn't protect him from getting frostbite on his nose when running in -40°C.

 ADVENTURE INSPIRATION

## HOW TO RUN IN STYLE

- Run to a local historical site dressed as a character from years gone by (think the Vikings, Romans, Tudors or Victorians).

- Head out for a spooky run dressed as a ghoul or a ghost for Halloween. Trick-or-treat along the way!

- Get someone to hide Easter eggs on your running route. Head out dressed as the Easter Bunny and hunt down the chocolate eggs one by one.

- You could get sponsorship from friends and family and do your run for charity.

# 9. SPEND THE NIGHT IN A WILDERNESS HUT

Wilderness huts are often in remote places and either have very basic facilities or none at all. That means you get to practise useful adventure skills, such as collecting water, using a shovel (to bury your poo) and gathering wood for a fire.

Seeking out and sleeping in a wilderness hut is always exciting. You'll get a nervous fizz in your belly when you round a bend and discover a simple building set in the middle of a towering forest, on the side of a mountain or deep in a lush green valley. Not knowing who you might meet at the hut is all part of the fun and you can make new friends for the night.

When you hike back to civilization after a hut adventure, it'll feel like you've just returned from a paradise in the wild. It's up to you to decide if you want to tell others about the hut or keep it as your secret...

# HOW TO DO IT

1. Take a tent or bivvy bag with you as back-up in case the hut is full. Huts work on a first-come, first-served basis, so whoever gets there first gets the beds!

2. Some wilderness huts can get busy on a weekend, so think about sneaking to one with your family in the middle of the week, especially in the school holidays.

3. Even though there will be four walls to protect you from the elements, the huts don't have heating, so bring warm clothes, a hat and some thick socks.

4. When it gets dark, it's unlikely you'll have electricity, so a torch is essential. Play cards and board games or tell stories by candlelight.

5. Remember to leave the hut clean and tidy. Take your rubbish with you and if there is no toilet and you have to bury your poo, do it well away from the water supply.

# AROUND THE WORLD

## WILDERNESS HUT NAMES

- Backcountry hut (New Zealand)

- Bothy (UK)

- Cabin (Norway)

- Mountain hut (USA)

- *Rifugio/Refuge* (France/Italy/Austria)

# 10. GO ON A SKATEBOARDING JOURNEY

Skateboarding is a fantastic way to travel because it's faster than walking – as well as a whole lot more fun – and less complicated than cycling. There are no pedals or gears to worry about, just the board, your body and the wind on your face. There are different types of skateboard you can choose for your journey – depending how far you want to go and how many tricks you want to do on the way!

### PENNYBOARD
**Best for:** learning to skate and simple tricks

### STANDARD SKATEBOARD
**Best for:** medium distances and more advanced tricks

### WHEN YOU GROW UP
Dave Cornthwaite skated 3,618 miles across the entire width of Australia. By the time Dave reached his destination five months later, he had used his right leg to push off 2,911,500 times, had worn through fourteen right shoes and had one massive calf muscle!

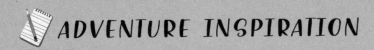

# ADVENTURE INSPIRATION

## DECIDE THE DISTANCE

Work out how far you think you can skateboard in a day. Do a few day trips first to test this out. You'll likely want to stick to less than 10 miles per day, to make sure you have some energy left and don't fall face first into your dinner each night.

## PICK A ROUTE

Unless you're planning to attach rocket boosters to your board, stick to flat, traffic-free pathways so that you can zoom effortlessly along. On a map look for old railway lines or pathways beside rivers, which tend to be flat.

## TAKE A COMPANION

Decide who you want to travel with on your journey: friends, a parent or siblings. It's best to go with people who are up for doing the same distance as you so that one of you isn't always waiting for the others!

## PACK LIGHT

Decide where you will sleep each night (a tent, bivvy or hostel) as this will affect how much gear you need to carry. Whatever you decide, only pack the bare essentials for your journey. You don't want to be tipping backwards off your board because your backpack weighs as much as a baby elephant. And, of course, don't forget your helmet!

## LONGBOARD
**Best for:** covering large distances quickly

# 11. LEARN TO WINDSURF

Harnessing nature's power is an incredible feeling. It's like flying – and windsurfing is one of the best ways to experience that sensation. It's an art, as both the wind and waves can be unpredictable, so you'll need all your strength and concentration to keep control of your board and sail. But once you've spent a day with aching arms, a salt-sprayed face and sun-bleached hair, you'll be hooked on racing through the waves.

## ✳ HOW TO DO IT

1. Find a local place to hire out a wetsuit and windsurf board. This could be a beachside club or a water-sports centre on a lake.

2. If you can, book a lesson with an instructor. There's a lot you can teach yourself but starting with good technique will make it easier in the long run.

3. Get the right gear. Make sure you hire a special "rig" (sail and board) for your size, and find a wetsuit that fits snugly too.

4. Get confident standing upright and holding the sail. If you do fall off, at least you'll have learned not to stand on that particular part of your board again!

5. Learn about wind direction and how to position your board and sail so you don't sail into an area of the wind called the No Go Zone.

6. Start small and build up your distances gradually. Begin by trying to sail between markers, then progress to more advanced courses.

# 12. LEARN TO KITESURF

You are whooshing across the waves, feeling like you have the ocean entirely to yourself. You feel free and alive – you are kitesurfing!

The first major challenge with kitesurfing is to understand how the wind behaves. Start by flying a large kite in your garden or local park on a windy day and feel how it moves with the wind. This will give you confidence and make your progress faster on the water.

Then find an instructor and hire a kitesurfing board. It's great to learn as a family because kitesurfing has nothing to do with strength and size – it's about understanding the wind and being skilful at handling the kite. You'll be showing your parents how it's done in no time!

Remember that falling off the board is to be expected. The more you crash, the more you learn! Be patient with your progress and know that if you just keep going, you will get better with time. Soon you'll be doing tricks and flips in the waves.

## AROUND THE WORLD

### WHERE TO CATCH THE WIND AND WAVES

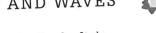

- Atins, Brazil
- Cape Hatteras, USA
- Dahab, Egypt
- Lake Garda, Italy
- Tiree, UK

# 13. VISIT A NATURAL WONDER OF THE WORLD

You can find beauty anywhere you look (starting with your back garden or local park), but there are some natural places around the world which deserve a special mention. These sights are so beautiful that if you're lucky enough to visit them, you'll be left open-mouthed in awe.

If you can't visit these sights, fear not. You can find other places nearer to you that are so incredible that they need to be protected and preserved. Look on a map for national parks, wilderness areas and UNESCO World Heritage Sites. Visit those and enjoy their awesomeness!

ADVENTURE

## GRAND CANYON (USA)

The Colorado River began carving out this canyon millions of years ago. Today in some places it is up to 18 miles across and 1,800 metres deep.

## GREAT BARRIER REEF (AUSTRALIA)

This 1,400-mile-long coral reef is bursting with all kinds of marine life.

## GUANABARA BAY (BRAZIL)

The deepest natural bay in the world has 130 pointy islands, the most famous being Sugarloaf Mountain.

## MOUNT EVEREST (NEPAL AND CHINA)

The highest mountain in the world stands at a whopping 8,848 metres above sea level.

## NORTHERN LIGHTS (ARCTIC CIRCLE)

Watch as cosmic space particles collide with the Earth's atmosphere and create a magical light show in the sky.

## PARÍCUTIN (MEXICO)

A 200-metre-wide cinder cone volcano which, over the course of a nine-year eruption, spewed molten lava onto the landscape around it.

## VICTORIA FALLS (ZAMBIA AND ZIMBABWE)

Watch the waters of the Zambezi River plunge 108 metres in the world's most spectacular waterfall.

TRAVEL

TICKET

POSTCARD

wish you were here!!

WON

*To visit

1. grand cany

2. great

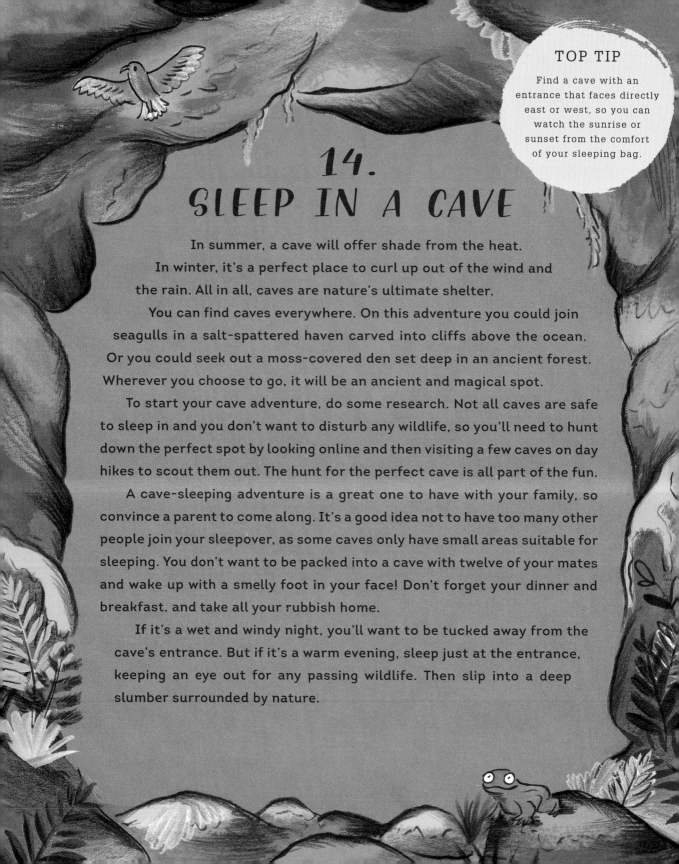

## TOP TIP

Find a cave with an entrance that faces directly east or west, so you can watch the sunrise or sunset from the comfort of your sleeping bag.

# 14.
# SLEEP IN A CAVE

In summer, a cave will offer shade from the heat. In winter, it's a perfect place to curl up out of the wind and the rain. All in all, caves are nature's ultimate shelter.

You can find caves everywhere. On this adventure you could join seagulls in a salt-spattered haven carved into cliffs above the ocean. Or you could seek out a moss-covered den set deep in an ancient forest. Wherever you choose to go, it will be an ancient and magical spot.

To start your cave adventure, do some research. Not all caves are safe to sleep in and you don't want to disturb any wildlife, so you'll need to hunt down the perfect spot by looking online and then visiting a few caves on day hikes to scout them out. The hunt for the perfect cave is all part of the fun.

A cave-sleeping adventure is a great one to have with your family, so convince a parent to come along. It's a good idea not to have too many other people join your sleepover, as some caves only have small areas suitable for sleeping. You don't want to be packed into a cave with twelve of your mates and wake up with a smelly foot in your face! Don't forget your dinner and breakfast, and take all your rubbish home.

If it's a wet and windy night, you'll want to be tucked away from the cave's entrance. But if it's a warm evening, sleep just at the entrance, keeping an eye out for any passing wildlife. Then slip into a deep slumber surrounded by nature.

# 15. GO GORGE-WALKING

Scramble, slip and slide your way back through time by venturing deep into a gorge: a narrow valley with steep rocky walls. Then prepare to get wet as you follow a route carved out thousands of years ago by a raging river.

Book a guide who can show you how to pick your way down moss-covered waterfalls and jump into icy plunge pools. Test your nerve by whooshing down rock slides – which are way more awesome than anything you'd ever find at a water park. Just don't forget your wetsuit as you'll get chilly in the water.

# 16. CYCLE BETWEEN TWO PLACES WITH THE SAME LETTER

You are on a mission. You will not stop until you complete it, pedalling down unknown trails across the countryside, going boldly where no cyclist has gone before, because you are cycling between two places that begin with the same letter! The planning part of the adventure is essential to the experience and a great way to discover your local area.

 ## HOW TO DO IT

1. Get a map of your local area and look for two places that begin with the same letter. Be creative: look for villages, towns, streets or landmarks. You want your route to be 3–6 miles between each place (a total of 6–12 miles if you are cycling there and back again).

2. Pick small roads or, better still, find cycle trails. Having less traffic around will make it a more relaxing ride.

3. Enjoy the ride! Make sure you allow time to fully immerse yourself in what the places you're cycling between have to offer, such as landmarks, museums – or ice-cream vans.

# 17. BIVVY OUT IN THE WILD

Imagine sleeping in a bedroom with no ceiling and no walls. You are warm and dry, but you can feel a cool breeze on your face. If you wake in the middle of the night, you'll open your eyes to a thousand twinkling stars.

Sleeping out in a bivvy bag gives you the fun of camping, but without the hassle of putting up a tent. A bivvy bag is a bit like a rain jacket for your sleeping bag: it slides over the top, making the sleeping bag waterproof and keeping you warm inside too. Once you're in the bivvy bag, that's it! You're all set for a great night's sleep under the stars.

## TOP TIP

There is nothing more fab than waking up, boiling a hot drink and enjoying it as you watch the sun rise, all while still snuggled in your bivvy bag. It's the best kind of breakfast in bed!

## HOW TO DO IT

1. Half the fun of sleeping outside is that you can chat away when you're tucked up in bed, so take some friends or family with you for company.

2. Choose a flat spot to bivvy on. If you sleep on even a slight hill, you'll find that you roll sideways or slide down it.

3. Slip both your camping mat and sleeping bag inside the bivvy. This will stop you sliding off the mat and waking up on the cold ground.

4. Bring a warm hat and scarf. Your head will be out of the bag for the night, so a good hat will keep you warm.

5. Turn your shoes upside down when you are going to sleep or put them in a waterproof bag next to you. This will stop them from getting wet.

6. Use your backpack as a pillow. That way, if it rains, you can pull the bivvy over the top of you and everything stays dry.

# 18. GO FOSSIL-HUNTING

Dinosaurs and woolly mammoths roamed the Earth many thousands of years ago, but you don't need to watch movies or go to a museum to see the remains of these creatures. Go fossil-hunting instead!

Fossils are the remains of once-living animals or plants that have been preserved in rock. They remain hidden until they are exposed by the elements. There's a real thrill in holding a piece of the prehistoric world in your palm and being reminded of the fascinating creatures - big and small - that were alive a long time before you were.

First you'll need to do some research on where there might be fossils nearby. Although there are fossils everywhere, they will be easier to find in certain places, such as beaches. Once you're at your fossil-hunting spot, be patient. Train your eyes to look closely at the shape of the rocks as you work your way around the site. It might be your lucky day! Always check that you're allowed to take home any discoveries.

## WHEN YOU GROW UP

Mary Anning was born in 1799 and is one of the greatest fossil-hunters ever to have lived. Her incredible finds include a plesiosaur and an ichthyosaur.

## AROUND THE WORLD

### FOSSIL-HUNTING LOCATIONS

- Big Brook Park, USA
- Borre, Denmark
- Joggins Fossil Cliffs, Canada
- Jurassic Coast, UK
- Western Cape, South Africa

# 19. TAKE A SLEEPER TRAIN

Wouldn't it be incredible if you could travel the world while you sleep? That's exactly what happens on a sleeper-train adventure. Clamber aboard just as it gets dark, snuggle down in a comfy bed and travel hundreds of miles, before waking up to a tasty breakfast in a completely new city or country. Better still, take a friend with you for the ultimate sleepover, but make sure you pick a friend who doesn't snore!

# AROUND THE WORLD

## MAKE GOING TO BED AN ADVENTURE

- 🌍 Chicago to San Francisco, USA: Go back in time when you spend two nights aboard the *California Zephyr*. Keep your eyes peeled for the ghosts of bandits as you pass through Gold Rush country and in and out of tunnels through the snow-capped Rocky Mountains.

- 🌍 London, England, to Fort William, Scotland: This 12-hour journey will take you from the skyscrapers of London to the lochs and mountains of the Scottish Highlands.

- 🌍 Moscow, Russia, to Nice, France: All aboard for a journey through eight European countries on a train that reaches speeds of up to 125 miles per hour! Go to sleep in Russia's capital city and wake up in France on the shores of the bright blue Mediterranean sea.

- 🌍 Trondheim to Bodø, Norway: Pack your winter woollies for this 10-hour journey through forests, mountains and fjords, all the way to the Arctic Circle (not far from the North Pole). If you're lucky, you might get elk sausage for breakfast.

- 🌍 Kapiri Mposhi, Zambia, to Dar es Salaam, Tanzania: Spend not one but two nights aboard a TAZARA train on this adventure. During the day, look out of the window and try to spot elephants, rhinos, hippos, lions, giraffes and zebras.

# 20. LEARN TO ROW

You can travel huge distances very quickly by rowing. The big, strong muscles in your legs and back can propel you for hours on end. Lots of people like to row alone, but often it's more fun with a team – and you'll go faster too.

Think about joining a local rowing club, or find an adult willing to take you out on the water for the first time. What type of boat you learn to row in will depend on where you intend to row. Ocean boats are bigger and more robust, whereas river boats are slim and built for speed. It's a good idea to start your rowing adventures on calm, flat water to practise your technique.

Once you're confident with your technique, decide where you'd like your rowing adventure to take you. Do you want to journey down a river for a picnic or head up a canal, from one lock to the next? Or do you have your eyes set on rowing out from shore and round a brightly coloured buoy bobbing out in the sea?

### WHEN YOU GROW UP
The Coxless Crew spent 257 days (almost nine months) rowing 8,446 miles across the Pacific Ocean from San Francisco, USA, to Cairns, Australia.

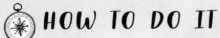

# HOW TO DO IT

Oar

Slide

Seat

Footplate

**TOP TIP**

When you first start rowing, you tend to grip the oar handles tightly, but this can lead to very sore wrists. Imagine that each oar handle is an egg – hold them with a loose but firm grip and don't crack that egg!

1. Find a place where you can try rowing – a boat club on a nearby river is a good place to start. See if you can sign up for a lesson with a coach so you can master the basics.

2. Before going out on the water, make sure you're wearing tight-fitting clothing. You don't want to get your oar handles tangled up in your T-shirt, or your shorts stuck in the slide.

3. When you get into the boat, put your foot in the space between the two seat slides and gently lower yourself down onto the seat. The bottom of a rowing boat is very fragile and if you stand there for too long, you might end up going through the boat!

4. Get your coach to ease you away from the riverbank. When you are on the water, wiggle the oars to see how that can affect the balance. What happens to the boat when you move one oar handle higher, then lower?

5. Rowing happens in two phases: the push and the recovery. Think of these as the push and the whoosh! The push stage is when you drive the boat forwards. In the recovery stage you move your arms and body and then slide as you prepare for the next stroke. When you're not rowing, rest your oar blades flat on the water to help you stay balanced (and upright!).

6. Rowing is a funny sport because you face away from the direction of travel. You'll need to get used to glancing over your shoulder every now and then to make sure you're not going to run over an unsuspecting duck or crash into other people on the water!

# 21. GO ON A FLIP-A-COIN ADVENTURE

It's time to fly by the seat of your adventure pants with this flip-a-coin adventure! You can do it wherever you are. All you need is a family member for an hour or two. First decide on the starting point for your adventure. It could be a local landmark, your school gates, your front door or your nearest park. Make sure you have a coin with you, as it will be your chief decision-making tool. Each time you get to a junction, stop and flip the coin to decide between left and right. Keep doing this at every junction you come to for an hour and just … go with the flow. There's a thrill in not knowing what you might find around the next bend.

Once you've got the hang of a flip-a-coin adventure, try mixing things up. You could do the same adventure cycling, scootering, skateboarding or rollerblading over a morning or afternoon, so you can explore an even bigger area.

# 22. LEARN TO SLACKLINE

Nothing will improve your balance skills like tip-toeing across a slackline. A slackline is a narrow strip of material that is stretched between two points, so you can walk across it. Or rather ... try to! Learning to slackline involves huge amounts of concentration, plenty of falling off, a fair amount of giggling and a real sense of satisfaction if you manage to stay on the line.

Set up the slackline between two trees in your garden or local park. It's a good idea to begin barefoot so you can feel the line beneath your feet. Try to keep the line underneath the middle of your foot and make sure you control your breathing. Even balancing on the line and breathing deeply is great practice. The slower you breathe, the less you'll wobble!

Once you can get across the line from one tree to the other (this might take a few weeks), set some challenges. Try tricks such as balancing on one leg or crouching down and standing up again. Can you stay on the line?

### WHEN YOU GROW UP
Highlining is like slacklining, but at a height. The Flying Frenchies, a group of highline artists, were the first people to take on the dangerous feat of walking a highline strung between two hot-air balloons in the sky!

# 23. GO CLIMBING

Have you ever spent a day outdoors and the hours have just flown by? Being on a climbing adventure is a completely absorbing experience. As you scale a wall or rock face, you're thinking so hard about your next move that you have no sense of time passing. When you do stop and look around, you'll see the world from an incredible new perspective.

In traditional climbing ropes are used to provide assistance, whereas in free climbing ropes are only used to stop the climber from falling. In solo climbing no ropes are used at all! To get started, you'll need to find a place to learn and an instructor too. If you live in a town or city, this will be an indoor climbing wall (these are great places to learn), but you could always begin with outdoor climbing if there's a good spot nearby.

 ## HOW TO DO IT

1. When you're standing at the bottom of a rock face, it might look big and scary. Remember that it will get easier once you are actually climbing. The best route will reveal itself as you go along.

2. It's all about the feet! Climbing shoes will give you extra control. Focus on looking for small steps from foothold to foothold on the wall and your hands will naturally work out where to go. You want to avoid pulling yourself up with your arms as they will quickly tire. Think more about your balance and less about using brute strength.

3. Trust your equipment! Climbing ropes are so strong that you could hang a four-by-four car from them. Unless you weigh more than a four-by-four, you don't have to worry about the rope not being able to hold your weight. You can also use chalk to give your hands extra grip.

4. Take things at your own pace. You have all the time in the world when you're climbing. It's not a race and you're there to enjoy the experience. Only go as far or as high as you want to.

5. Some days when you go climbing it will feel really tough, and then other days ... wham! Everything will just slot into place. The difficult days are just progress towards the days when you will float effortlessly up the wall.

## WHEN YOU GROW UP

Maureen "Mo" Beck was born without her lower left arm. She started climbing when she was twelve and is now a competitive paraclimber, a five-time national champion and a two-time world champion. She is passionate about getting more people into climbing.

## TOP TIP

Think about what water would look like flowing uphill. What path would it take? That's the way you want to climb – taking the path of least resistance and flowing effortlessly, but with a quiet power.

# 24. JOURNEY TO WHERE YOUR GRANDPARENTS WERE BORN

You are one very special adventurer. There is no other human being on this planet just like you. But how much do you know about your family history? It's time to hop into a time machine and discover where your grandparents came from! Team up with your parents or siblings for this adventure.

Find out where your grandparents were born by asking your relatives and researching online. Then plan your journey with the help of your parents. If it's nearby can you cycle or walk to their birthplace? If it turns out your grandparents came from a long way away, read about that place and go on a virtual adventure instead.

# 25. TIE A BOWLINE KNOT

With tree platforms to build, rafts to make and boats to sail, knowing how to tie a strong knot is essential to your adventuring! A bowline is one of the most secure and useful knots you can learn, and once you've got the hang of it, it's super easy to tie and untie.

 ## HOW TO DO IT

1. Make a small loop in the rope, leaving a long tail at the end. Pass the tail of the rope under and through the loop. Bring the tail around the back of the top section of the rope.

 2. Bring the tail around to the front of the rope, and then pass the tail back through the small loop.

3. Tighten the knot by pulling the tail down and the top of the rope up.

# 26. TAKE A PHOTO EVERY DAY FOR A YEAR

Have you ever thought about how many memories you make in a whole year? There are so many new sights, sounds and smells you experience over 365 days. This adventure is about recording a little snapshot of each day for an entire year, so you can remember what you were doing and who you were with.

The only rule for this adventure is that each photo has to be taken outside. Come rain, shine, darkness or light, outside is where the photo-party is happening! Remember that you're just capturing a moment. It's a snapshot in time, so don't worry too much about setting the shot up to be perfect. When you look back on the year, you want to have a record of your adventures – the best bits, the worst bits and the muddy bits! If you enjoy yourself, maybe it's something you can carry on doing next year too.

## ADVENTURE INSPIRATION

### MAKE A SCRAPBOOK
Look for something outdoors that makes you smile each day. Take a photo of it. At the end of the year, print all 365 photos out and put them in a scrapbook so you can flick through your memories.

### MAKE A COLLAGE
Upload your 365 outdoor photos on to your computer and print them out so they are tiny. Cut them out and pop them in a big frame, so you can hang your year of adventure on the wall. You could arrange the photos month by month, season by season or just scatter them randomly.

### MAKE A MOVIE
Take the same selfie each day, but with a different background every time. Download a time-lapse app and run the selfies together to create a movie. Watch how your face changes over the course of a year.

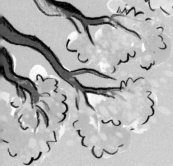

# 27. LEARN THE NAMES OF FOUR TREES

There's no two ways about it: trees are amazing! Learning about them is not only a way to impress your friends when you're out and about, it will also help you forage for food and choose firewood when you're on longer adventures. From the big and knobbly to the tall and slender, here are four incredible trees to discover in the wild.

 **SPOTTER'S GUIDE: TREES**

## OAK
**Look for:** acorns

**Great for:** climbing! There are lots of low-hanging branches to dangle from

**Grows naturally:** anywhere in the Northern Hemisphere with a cool climate

## WHITE WILLOW

**Look for:** slim, long leaves with white undersides and grey-brown bark with deep grooves

**Great for:** lazing underneath for a riverside picnic

**Grows naturally:** in the UK, Europe and western and central Asia

## ASPEN

**Look for:** short, wide leaves, narrow trunks and very knobbly twigs

**Great for:** making boat paddles! The wood of an aspen tree is lightweight but very strong so is often used for making things

**Grows naturally:** in the UK, Europe, Asia, Africa and the USA

## RAINBOW EUCALYPTUS

**Look for:** rainbow-coloured bark! New green bark gradually changes colour and the tree ends up with streaks of blue, purple, orange and dark red

**Great for:** making paper. The wood pulp made from the tree is the main ingredient in white paper

**Grows naturally:** in Indonesia, Papua New Guinea and the Philippines

# 28. GO ON A MULTI-DAY RUNNING JOURNEY

Running is a simple way to travel. All you need is a pair of trainers, some puff in your lungs and a willingness to explore. You can get off the beaten track - down long-forgotten forest pathways, across windswept hilltops and through wildflower meadows - all the places in the world that cars and bikes can't go. Your feet will be pounding on the ground, but your head will be in the clouds and the adrenaline will be pumping through your veins. You will feel INVINCIBLE!

It's important that you pace yourself. On a long run, you should always have enough breath to talk when you're running - that means you're at a steady speed you can maintain for hours. Stop every 30-45 minutes to have a stretch and something to eat and drink. Don't wait until you're hungry or thirsty - that's too late!

## WHEN YOU GROW UP
Rosie Swale-Pope ran 20,000 miles around the world. It was the longest unsupported solo run in history. She pulled everything she needed in a small cabin on wheels that doubled up as a place for her to sleep each night.

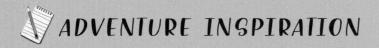

# ADVENTURE INSPIRATION

## DECIDE YOUR DISTANCE

How far do you want to run each day? If you're new to running, up to 10 kilometres per day will allow for some great exploring.

## CHOOSE YOUR ROUTE

Think about what kind of scenery you want to run through. Would you like to explore historic sites like old castles? Or perhaps you'd prefer to see a lake or river? How about running alongside waves crashing into a rugged coastline? Tailor the route to what you want to see because the more you love the scenery, the more it'll spur you on. National trails make great routes and often have maps available online.

## PLAN YOUR SUPPLIES

If there are lots of little towns en route, then you won't need to carry much food or water, but if you're heading into the wilderness, pack some sandwiches.

## FIND A PLACE TO SLEEP

Are you going to stay in a tent or a hostel? If you opt for a tent you can ask an adult running with you to carry it and other essentials.

# 29. TRACE A RIVER FROM SOURCE TO SEA

A journey along a river will take you from a tiny trickle at the source all the way to the sea. Look on a map to find a small spring that feeds a bigger river and then follow it to the ocean.

You'll never know what's around the next bend on this adventure. Perhaps you'll stop to meet the people who live in the towns and cities along the river's banks? Or maybe you'll forge onwards, just like the water, gathering speed as it crashes through rapids, sneaks between gorges, tumbles over waterfalls and finally whooshes out to sea.

One of the best things about this adventure is that you can choose how you want to travel. You could opt for a stand-up paddleboard or propel yourself a little faster in a kayak or rowing boat. You could swim part of the distance. Or you could travel beside the river by running, walking or cycling along the bank.

## WHEN YOU GROW UP
Lindsey Cole chose a unique way to travel for her source-to-sea adventure down the River Thames. She wore a nude wetsuit and a mermaid's tail and "mermaided" her way along the river, in a bid to raise awareness about plastic pollution.

## AROUND THE WORLD

### EPIC RIVERS

- 🌍 Thames, UK: 215 miles
- 🌍 Ganges, India: 1,569 miles
- 🌍 Danube, Europe: 1,771 miles
- 🌍 Mississippi, USA: 2,320 miles
- 🌍 Amazon, South America: 4,345 miles

# 30. TRAVEL TO WHERE YOUR FOOD COMES FROM

Have you ever thought about where the food on your plate comes from? Are you eating broccoli from Britain, chocolate from Ghana or bananas from Ecuador? Often we have no idea about the adventure our food has been on before it reaches our plates. It's fascinating to discover the origins of what we eat and this adventure could take you to far-flung forests, plantations on the other side of the planet – or perhaps to a farm down the road from your home.

## HOW TO DO IT

1. Start by listing the food you've eaten this week. Think about whether each thing was grown or made from combining different ingredients.

2. Pick three or four items, such as fruit, vegetables, meat or fish, and look at the packaging to find out where the food has come from.

3. If the food has come from nearby, talk to your family or teacher and see if you can visit the farm where it was grown or raised. If not, see if you can visit a nearby farm shop and discover what is grown in your local area and how it ends up on your plate.

4. For food that has come from further away, look at a map and work out how many thousands of miles it has travelled to get to you. Has it come by lorry, plane or boat? Could you visit that country one day?

# 31. READ A MAP

When you head out on an adventure, it might be tempting to use your phone or a GPS device to help you find your way. But not only is it very satisfying to be able to read a paper map, it is an important survival skill.

Learning how to read a map means that you take notice of the landscapes around you. You will know how many massive hills you need to climb simply by looking at your route! And besides, paper maps can't stop working in the rain or run out of battery ... you are all the power they need to come to life!

The first thing to learn with map-reading is how to identify what all the different lines, blobs, symbols and squiggles mean. Lay your map out on a table and look for the key, which can normally be found on the edges of the map. It will tell you the meaning of every symbol or line.

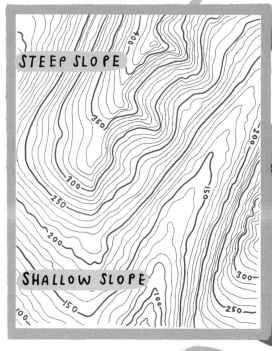

Once you've covered the basics, the next step is to get to grips with contour lines. The thin, wiggly lines show you how steep or high a hill is.

Imagine that the hill is made up of layers, like a cake. Each section of that hill (or layer of the cake) is marked with a line and a number to let you know how far above sea level it is. So if a section of the hill has a wiggly line and the number 280, that layer of the hill is 280 metres above sea level. When contour lines are close together, it means that the height of each layer is changing quickly, so the hill is steep.

When you've learned as much as you can by looking at a map indoors, it's time to head outside to put your skills to the test. Find an adult or older friend who is good at map-reading and head to an open area of land, where you can easily read the landscape and match what you see to where you are on the map. Look for defining features in the landscape, such as railway lines, hills, rivers and patches of woodland, and use them to find your position on the map.

# HOW TO DO IT

1. Look for the key on the edge of the map, which should tell you the meaning of each symbol.

2. Find each symbol on the map.

3. Maps are divided into boxes called grid squares. Now you know how a key works, ask an adult to point to a grid square and set a timer for 3 minutes.

4. Write down how many things you can see in that grid square, without checking the map's key. How many things have you written down by the end? You could do this in teams and make it a competition.

5. Now look at a map of the area near your home. Can you use your new knowledge to identify any local landmarks on the map?

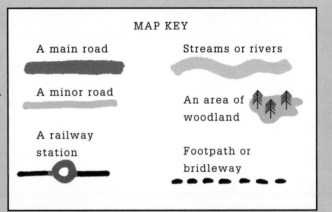

MAP KEY

A main road

A minor road

A railway station

Streams or rivers

An area of woodland

Footpath or bridleway

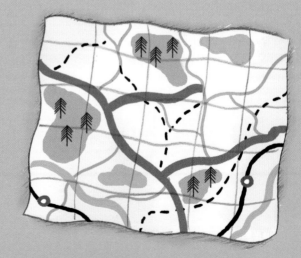

# 32. WRITE YOUR NAME BY WALKING THE STREETS

Add creativity to your adventures and make your mark on the world by walking around your local town or neighbourhood in a pattern that spells out your name. Try running, scooting or cycling so that you can cover more distance. You can also create more complex words or shapes – even animals.

 ## HOW TO DO IT

1. First you need to plot your route. Use an online map service, such as Google Maps, and locate your area.

2. Click along the streets to create your route, trying to use junctions as a way to spell your name. Try to make your route no longer than a few miles. Be patient as it is a little fiddly. This adventure is as much a mental challenge as it is a physical one!

3. Once you've created the route, upload it to your phone or GPS device.

4. Grab a parent and head out of the door, following the lines you've set yourself. As you walk, remember that if an alien was looking down from space at that very moment, you'd be drawing them a work of art!

# 33. GO ON A TRAIL RUN

Trail running will get you sweaty and muddy – the muddier the better! You'll bounce over puddles, pass through ancient forests and dash along windswept hilltops and stretches of sandy beach.

This adventure is kind to your body and mind. The soft earth of a trail is far easier on your legs than a hard pavement. And you'll be so distracted by your amazing surroundings that you won't notice the distance passing!

Look for established paths or old railway lines in your area. If you live in a city, a riverside towpath or a local park will give you a trail-running taster. You could start with an organized event on an easy trail, such as a parkrun, and then find your own routes further afield.

Break the distance down by looking out for landmarks. Think about running to the next tree or bush and the distance will whizz by in no time at all. Start with 1 kilometre and then gradually build up to 5 kilometres.

If you fall in love with trail running, don't forget you can turn your adventure into a multi-day running journey. See Adventures 28 and 64 for more ideas.

## TOP TIP

Choose trainers with grip that will help you keep your footing in sloppy conditions. And depending on your natural running style, you might need to pick your feet up more than usual to avoid tripping over the uneven ground.

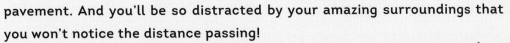

# 34. HIKE THE SAME TRAIL IN FOUR SEASONS

One of the best things about adventuring is that you can revisit a place over and over again, yet have a completely different experience every time depending on who you're with, what the weather is like and even what you had for breakfast. No two days outside are ever the same, so why not walk the same trail in spring, summer, autumn and winter?

Trails with lots of plants and trees are best for this adventure, because they will change from one season to the next. On your map, look for forests and nature reserves to help you find the most interesting routes. Take a photo of the trail in each season and look back at just how much it's changed over time.

# 35. GO WILD SWIMMING

For a refreshing adventure, plunge into a wild swimming pool. Float gently down a river under a bright blue sky, bob around in a lake surrounded by forest, or body-surf along waves in the ocean. Unlike your local swimming pool, wild swimming spots are often deserted, so you can splash and swim for hours with only the birds and fish for company.

Wild swimming always feels adventurous because you never quite know what the water will be like. It could be too deep or cold to be right for swimming. You should never swim alone and always with an adult's supervision. It's important to test the current before you swim too. You can do this by throwing a stick in. If it moves fast, don't go in and save your swim for another day.

## TOP TIP

Don't just wait for the sun to come out! Cold water dips send blood whooshing around your body and make you feel on top of the world. Just keep your swim short and make sure you have warm clothes to pull on afterwards.

# 36. HAVE A SEAWEED SUPPER

Fancy a seaweed sandwich? Seaweed isn't just something that tickles your toes when you're swimming in the sea. It's one of the most delicious and nutritious food sources on the planet. Best of all, you won't need to part with a penny because ... foraging for seaweed is free!

Foraging is a great way to add another dimension to your adventuring - not only are you looking and listening to the world around you, you're tasting it too. With hundreds of types of edible seaweed, and different species growing depending on the season, you'll be spoilt for choice.

When foraging, you need to take an adult with you who knows what to look for. Once harvested, throw the seaweed in your dinner and cook it right away, like you would fresh veg, or dry it out for a few months in a jar and sprinkle over other meals for extra flavour.

 **SPOTTER'S GUIDE: SEAWEED**

### SEA LETTUCE
**Taste:** spicy, salty and crunchy

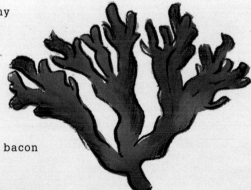

### DULSE
**Taste:** just like bacon

## KELP
**Taste:** sweet, salty and smoky

## SEA SPAGHETTI
**Taste:** beefy, nutty and salty (and chewy!)

## GUT WEED
**Taste:** salty

## PEPPER DULSE
**Taste:** fresh and garlicky

# 37. RIDE A HORSE

Riding long distances on horseback allows you to travel slowly and quietly over mountain passes, across rivers, along beaches and through forests. This means you can explore off the beaten track and experience sights you might miss if you were on a bike or in a car.

But before you can go on big adventures in the wilderness, you need to get confident riding a horse. Find a riding school nearby, with a teacher who can introduce you to a new horse and show you how to ride it. City farms often have riding clubs too.

Learning how to ride a horse is very different from surfing, kayaking or cycling because the key piece of equipment (your horse) is a living being that has a mind of its own, just like you! Therefore, the first step is making friends with your horse. The best way to do that is to relax and be yourself. Horses are very sensitive and will pick up on your fear. If you're relaxed, the horse will relax too.

When you first visit a stable, don't expect to start riding straight away. Get to know your horse by grooming it or tacking up (putting on the saddle, reins and harness). These activities will help you to bond with the horse, so when you do start riding, you'll already be great friends.

### WHEN YOU GROW UP

Can you imagine horseriding across the world? That's what Megan Lewis did when she spent four years riding thousands of miles from China back to her home in the UK. She completed her journey on several different horses.

# HOW TO DO IT

1. Whenever you ride make sure that you have a hat (with chin strap), a body protector, gloves and boots. Make sure you wear boots without laces, as you don't want them getting stuck in the stirrups (the metal platforms for your feet) if you fall off!

2. Sit up tall in the saddle with a foot in each stirrup. Stay relaxed and move your body in sync with the horse. This will keep the load light for the horse and keep you in control.

3. Hold the reins gently. They are connected to a bit in the horse's mouth and if you pull on them hard, you might hurt the horse. You can stop the horse by pulling very gently on the reins.

4. To move to the right, press your left calf into the horse's side and move the right rein out to the right. To move to the left, press your right calf and move your left rein to the left.

5. When you have mastered the basics, you can move on to trotting and cantering – and even galloping and jumping.

# 38. GO ON A
# NIGHT-TIME HIKE

Imagine hiking through darkened woods and along blustery hilltops, guided by the light of a silver moon. It could be a warm summer's evening or the depths of frosty winter. Either way there is something magical about an adventure after dark with a group of friends, when your senses are heightened and familiar things suddenly look different. It's a good idea to pick a route that you've walked during the daytime so you don't get lost. It won't guarantee that you don't step in a GIANT cowpat – you'll just have to take that risk!

If you prefer to hike in total darkness (when the stars are easier to see), then pick a time in the lunar cycle when the moon is a new moon or crescent moon. But if you like a lot of natural light (when the trail is easier to see), then head out on a full moon. Either way, always take an adult with you and a good torch (or head torch) and spare batteries.

Hills in or around cities or towns are great places to head at night-time too. There's something satisfying about looking down on a mass of twinkling lights, knowing everyone else is doing normal indoor things while you're out exploring under a blanket of darkness.

 ADVENTURE INSPIRATION

## ADD AN EXTRA ELEMENT TO YOUR ADVENTURE

- See how many nocturnal animals you can hear or see on your hike: look out for hedgehogs, owls, bats and foxes.

- Combine your hike with a spot of stargazing (see Adventure 39).

- End your hike at a graveyard and tell spooky stories (see Adventure 76).

# 39. GO STARGAZING

When you look at stars in the sky, you are seeing light that has been emitted from fiery balls of exploding gas millions of miles away. Wowsers!

Sailors use stars to navigate and with a little practice, you can learn to tell exactly where you are in the world by looking at the stars. There are eighty-eight collections of stars, known as constellations, spread out across the night sky. The constellations form a spectacular map of mythical creatures and heroic warriors, just waiting to be revealed. Stargazing is never boring because the more you look, the more you'll see. Learning the story behind each constellation is as much fun as trying to identify it in the first place.

If you really enjoy stargazing, then you could invest in a simple telescope to allow you to see more. And the next step could be to take a trip to your nearest observatory to look at the sky through a really powerful telescope.

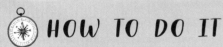 ## HOW TO DO IT

1. Find a stargazing spot. If you live in a town or city then the light from streetlamps and houses might prevent you from seeing the stars. The best places to go stargazing are miles from any source of artificial light. The countryside or the desert are ideal.

2. Get up high. Stargazing from the top of a local hill or mountain will allow you to see more of the night sky.

3. Choose a time in the lunar cycle when the moon is less full and therefore less bright. It'll mean the constellations are easier to spot.

4. Use a star map in a book or an app and learn to identify one or two particular constellations.

# 40. FLOAT DOWN A RIVER

When the sun is shining, sometimes it's nice to just kick back, relax and go with the flow. Grab some friends, push off from the riverbank and let the natural current of the water take you downstream.

You'll need something that floats for this adventure – and make sure it's a reasonable size. A rubber ring, a stand-up paddleboard, a raft or an inflatable unicorn will all work. Choose a quiet section of river where the flow is slow and you know there are lots of places to get out along the bank. Even though you will be floating, bring a small paddle so you can direct your vessel if you need to. You can wear a wetsuit and old shoes if you want added protection.

Take an adult with you and make sure there is someone to collect you at the other end (you can't float back upstream). They can bring a picnic for everyone to enjoy.

# 41. CATCH AND COOK YOUR DINNER

If you ever found yourself stranded near a river or the sea, would you be able to catch and cook something for dinner? Even if you're not in a survival situation, there's something very satisfying about spending all day fishing outdoors, and then cooking your supper on an open fire.

## HOW TO DO IT

1. You need a guide who can lend you the right equipment, show you the best way to catch a fish and make sure your fishing is sustainable. The fish population needs to be strong and healthy in your chosen spot, so there's enough fish for your fellow adventurers in years to come.

2. Once you begin, be patient. Fishing is as much about spending time outdoors with family or friends as it is about catching something. You may get a bite on your line within 20 minutes. Other times you may have to wait all day.

3. When you've caught a fish, prepare yourself for some guts and slime! Catching a fish is all well and good, but to be a fully-fledged catch 'n' cooker, you'll need to learn how to gut and clean the fish. Watch your guide show you how it is done.

4. Cook your fish on the embers of a campfire. Wrap it in foil with some lemon slices and place it on the embers for 10–12 minutes. Unwrap and enjoy your dinner!

# 42. GO SNORKELLING

The underwater world is a magical place. A simple snorkel and mask allow you to explore what happens beneath the waves and you might see colourful fish or rainbow coral. But remember that you don't have to live near the ocean to go snorkelling. You can snorkel anywhere there is water: rivers, lakes – even swimming pools.

**WHEN YOU GROW UP**
How about taking part in the World Bog Snorkelling Championships? Every year, a group of snorkel-lovers swim their way through narrow, muddy streams, often wearing fancy dress. There's no time for wildlife-spotting — it's the fastest bog snorkeller who will claim the champion's crown!

# HOW TO DO IT

1. Try to snorkel in calm, shallow waters, where the water is clear and there are fewer waves. Make sure an adult is swimming with you.

2. Start by dunking your head in and out of the water wearing just the face mask. You want to make sure the mask is watertight and that there's nothing trapped around the edges (such as your hair).

3. Attach your snorkel pipe and breathe normally through the mouthpiece. Relax! Don't hold your breath.

4. Don't try to use your arms to swim like you normally would. Let them float alongside your body and gently use your feet to move forwards. This will keep your head still and help you get the best view.

5. Borrow some flippers for your feet. Wearing flippers increases the surface area of your feet, meaning that when you move them in the water they will propel you further and faster.

6. As you become more confident, practise taking a deep breath and holding it as you dive down. When you come back above the surface, blow out hard and shoot any water in your snorkel tube into the air like a whale!

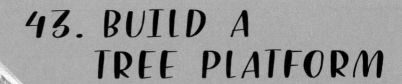

# 43. BUILD A TREE PLATFORM

Building a tree platform is more straightforward than building a tree house, but just as fun. It takes time, though, and you'll need an adult's help, so this isn't an adventure for a single afternoon. Start by choosing your tree and then researching different types of platforms. Remember to design your platform so that it is supported by the tree's existing branches and doesn't restrict the tree's growth. Once you start building, it's likely that you'll end up with a platform that's different from the one you first imagined! Problem-solving is all part of the fun and every bit of effort you put in will be worth it in the end. Soon, you'll have your very own hideout, up high in the sky, where you can hang out with your friends, hold secret meetings and see the birds and squirrels up close.

## ADVENTURE INSPIRATION

### CHOOSE THE RIGHT TREE
Work out if there's a tree in your garden or a family member's garden that can hold a platform. You want a tree with a wide and straight trunk. Also look at the branches. An even spread of thick branches will give you lots of options for support points for your platform.

### DESIGN THE STRUCTURE
The main beams will form the basic shape of your platform and should be set in a square shape across strong tree branches. They will act as your foundation. The supporting beams will go between the main beams and give the platform extra support.

### FINISH WITH A FUNKY FLOOR
The floor of your platform will be made of wooden slats, which you can customize by painting them funky colours or drawing on them.

# 44. GO SAILING

A new adventure is often both hard work and amazing fun. Learning to sail is just that: it's tricky at first, but once you get the hang of it, you'll never look back. You'll need to learn how to read the wind in order to plot your course and then how to navigate the boat across the water. You'll also need to know your knots, so you'd best get practising your bowline (see Adventure 25), clove hitch, rolling hitch and reef knot.

There are many different types of sailing boat, but light and nimble dinghy boats are great for learning, because you can see the effects of your movement on the boat immediately. You can rent dinghies from water-sports centres on rivers or lakes, where you'll find an instructor to show you the basics too. You'll be whooshing over waves and back to shore in no time.

Where you go sailing is up to you. There are lakes, rivers and the sea to explore, but you can journey beyond the horizon, discovering remote islands or a new country. Yachts are big sailing boats, upwards of 10 metres long and sometimes as large as 180 metres! They need more crew members to sail them and are used for adventures further afield. If you live near the sea or have a friend or relative who often takes to the waves in a yacht, then you could learn the ropes by asking to join them. One day, you could sail around the world!

### WHEN YOU GROW UP
Geoff Holt is a disabled seafaring explorer and is the first quadriplegic sailor to sail unassisted across the Atlantic Ocean. He completed the 2,700-mile voyage in 28 days in a specially designed catamaran called *Impossible Dream*.

# 45. HIKE UP A HILL FOR A SUNRISE BREAKFAST

Look on a map and find a hill that has a good view of the eastern sky, where the sun rises in the morning. Make sure you've got warm layers and a good torch to light your way. Pack your bag with a top-notch breakfast, so you can enjoy it at the top, surrounded by the reds and pinks of sunrise. Magic!

# 46. GO ISLAND-HOPPING

Hopping from island to island is adventure paradise! Once upon a time these islands would have been part of the same mass of land, but now they're scattered into pieces across the ocean - just waiting for you to head out and explore them. On each new island you'll discover different plants, animals and ways of life. Decide how you'll travel between the islands. If they're not too far apart you could kayak, stand-up paddleboard or even swim. If they're further afield you might need to travel by ferry instead.

## AROUND THE WORLD

### INCREDIBLE ISLAND-HOPPING DESTINATIONS

- 🌍 Cyclades, Greece
- 🌍 Florida Keys, USA
- 🌍 Galápagos Islands, Ecuador
- 🌍 Lofoten Islands, Norway
- 🌍 Outer Hebrides, Scotland

# 47. GO BAREFOOT WANDERING

Did you know that there are 7,000 tingle-tastic nerve endings on the sole of each foot? Your feet are as sensitive as your hands, so don't keep them scrunched up in shoes when they could be having their own adventures! Start in your back garden. Slip off your shoes and see if you can feel a change beneath your soles. It will take a bit of time to get used to the sensation and you'll need to pay close attention to where you walk so you don't step on anything sharp. But once you've done it a few times, your soles will start to toughen up. Then you can try walking on sand, the forest floor, tarmac and pebbles.

# 48. LEAVE A TRAIL OF KINDNESS

Nothing gives you a warm, fuzzy feeling like doing something to help a fellow human. Being kind means putting in a bit of extra effort to help someone out. Even seemingly small acts of kindness can make a huge difference to that person's day and your own. And there's a magical law in the universe: the more kindness you spread, the more you'll receive.

 ADVENTURE INSPIRATION

## HOW TO LEAVE A TRAIL OF KINDNESS

- Wash a neighbour's car
- Tidy your grandparents' garden
- Help your parents do the family laundry
- Help a warden clean up a local park
- Help a friend with a school project
- Pick up fifty pieces of litter from your neighbourhood

# 49. LEARN TO STAND-UP PADDLEBOARD

If you love the idea of splashing around on a river, look no further than stand-up paddleboarding (SUP for short). Standing on the board gives you a 360-degree view of the wildlife and landscape, and you have enough control to paddle off and explore wherever you fancy. Even if you're not aiming to travel long distances, it's still a freeing and peaceful experience to paddle down a river or canal for an hour or two.

When you're learning, not knowing if you're going to fall off is all part of the fun. The struggle to stay upright adds to the satisfaction when you're finally able to cruise effortlessly along on your board.

## TOP TIP

It's better to take long sweeping strokes on the board, rather than short, sharp ones. This will keep the board moving along at a steady pace and stop you from getting too tired.

##  HOW TO DO IT

1. Find a place where you can hire a board and buoyancy aid for the day. This might be at a local lake, a beach or a water-sports centre. Go for a wide board to begin with.

2. Find a SUP instructor to teach you the first few times, and start on flat, calm water so that you can get your balance and fine-tune your paddling skills.

3. Start by kneeling and paddling. Then slowly stand up, staying in the middle of the board and keeping your feet parallel. Keep your knees slightly bent. Use your top arm to drive the paddle into the water and move forwards. Switch sides after a few strokes to stay in a straight line.

4. Then try the fun stuff: tricks on the board (such as handstands), or giving your friends rides while you paddle.

5. If you enjoy SUP, you could buy your own board, perhaps even one that's inflatable, so you can easily take it on adventures.

## WHEN YOU GROW UP

Imagine stand-up paddleboarding over 1,000 miles in four months, carrying everything you need on your board and meeting snakes, crocodiles, leopards, scorpions and elephants along the way! Kevin Brady adventured down Sri Lanka's Mahaweli River on a SUP and then around the island.

# 50. CYCLE UP A MOUNTAIN

Cycling is a faster way to get to the top of a mountain than walking. It comes with the added bonus that once you've taken in the hard-earned view from the summit, you get to freewheel effortlessly down the other side. *Wahoo!*

**WHEN YOU GROW UP**
Daniel Teklehaimanot was the first rider from an African team to win the King of the Mountains jersey in the Tour de France. It is awarded to the rider with the most points for hill-climbing — points are awarded for reaching the mountain summits first.

## AROUND THE WORLD

### PACE YOURSELF ON THESE CLIMBS

🌐 Box Hill, UK

🌐 Col du Tourmalet, France

🌐 Colorado National Monument, USA

🌐 Mount Haleakalā, USA

🌐 Paso Internacional los Libertadores, Argentina/Chile

# HOW TO DO IT

1. Look at a map to find a high point of land near you with a road that goes all the way to the top. If the road looks wiggly on the map, then that's a good sign. Wiggles usually mean that the gradient is less steep, which makes it easier to keep going on your bike.

2. Pack snacks, water and layers.

3. Settle into a steady rhythm from the foot of the climb and relax into the ride by finding a good gear on your bike. You want to be using the smaller gear cog (the circle with spiky teeth) at the front of the chain mechanism. You'll know you're in the right gear because you can move your legs continuously and still have some breath to be able to talk.

4. If you hit a really steep section, you may find that even in your easiest gear, your legs turn very slowly and there may be a stretch where you are puffing and panting. Grit your teeth, push hard on the pedals and keep going, no matter how slowly. You'll be so proud when you make it out of the steep section without having got off the bike.

5. At the top, pull on a few more layers of clothing, have something to eat and prepare for a glorious whizz all the way back down to the bottom.

# 51. LEARN TO COUNT TO TWENTY IN THREE DIFFERENT LANGUAGES

Adventuring isn't just about tiring out your body. It's also about getting your brain buzzing. New people, places, sights and smells all feed your mind. Challenge yourself by learning how to count from one to twenty in three different languages. Once you've got the numbers mastered, you can move on to learning a few phrases and then you'll be ready to chat to your new adventure friends.

 ## ADVENTURE INSPIRATION

| ENGLISH | FRENCH | POLISH | SPANISH |
|---------|---------|---------------|-----------|
| one | un | jeden | uno |
| two | deux | dwa | dos |
| three | trois | trzy | tres |
| four | quatre | cztery | cuatro |
| five | cinq | pięć | cinco |
| six | six | sześć | seis |
| seven | sept | siedem | siete |
| eight | huit | osiem | ocho |
| nine | neuf | dziewięć | nueve |
| ten | dix | dziesięć | diez |
| eleven | onze | jedenaście | once |
| twelve | douze | dwanaście | doce |
| thirteen | treize | trzynaście | trece |
| fourteen | quatorze | czternaście | catorce |
| fifteen | quinze | piętnaście | quince |
| sixteen | seize | szesnaście | dieciséis |
| seventeen | dix-sept | siedemnaście | diecisiete |
| eighteen | dix-huit | osiemnaście | dieciocho |
| nineteen | dix-neuf | dziewiętnaście | diecinueve |
| twenty | vingt | dwadzieścia | veinte |

**OTHER LANGUAGES TO TRY:**
Dutch, German, Icelandic, Italian, Mandarin, Portuguese, Swedish

# 52. PUT YOUR FINGER ON A MAP AND GO!

As an adventurer, you welcome the unknown with open arms. So why not take the mystery of an adventure to the next level: put your finger on a map and just … GO!

## HOW TO DO IT

1. Decide how you're going to travel to your (as yet) unknown location. Will you go on foot (running or walking), by bike, scooter, rollerblades or skateboard?

2. Decide how far you are willing to travel. Get a map of the local area and measure that distance from your location. Draw a circle with your house in the centre. This is your adventure radius!

3. Shut your eyes, hover over the map and try to put your finger somewhere within that circle. It might take a few goes!

4. Open your eyes and see where your finger has landed. That's your destination! Time to grab your family, head out of the door and GO!

# 53. SLEEP IN A HAMMOCK

Have you noticed how you often fall asleep if you're in a car or on a train? There's something about gentle motion that makes us sleepy and that's why a hammock is the perfect place to spend the night. Sling a hammock between two trees in a garden and gently rock yourself to sleep.

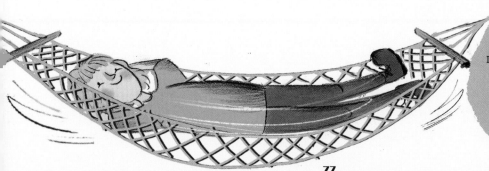

## TOP TIP

Don't pull the hammock too tight as it will make you more likely to fall out! It should sag in a "smile shape" between the two trees.

# 54. SEE YOUR FAVOURITE ANIMAL IN THE WILD

What's your favourite animal? Maybe it's a cat or a dog, a snake, a mouse or a chinchilla - something that you can keep as a pet in your home. But perhaps it's something a little wilder ... such as a giraffe or an elephant! Going to see an animal in its natural habitat is the ultimate wildlife adventure. It's fascinating to observe how each animal survives: what it hunts, where it sleeps and how it lives alongside other wildlife. You won't be able to interact with the animals - they're wild after all - but watching them in their natural environment will fill you with a sense of wonder for our world.

 SPOTTER'S GUIDE: WILD ANIMALS

## BLACK BEARS
Black bears live in forests. They're excellent tree climbers, great swimmers and can run at speeds of up to 30 miles per hour. You'll be able to spot them in many areas of North America, and especially if you head to Great Smoky Mountains National Park in Tennessee and North Carolina.

## ORCAS
Although orcas are often known as killer whales, they are actually a species of dolphin. They get their name from their amazing ability to catch other marine animals, including sea lions, dolphins and even whales. They are very social, living in large groups called pods. Go and see them off Vancouver Island in Canada.

## TIGERS

If you think that you can eat a lot of dinner, imagine eating 40 kilograms of meat in one sitting! That's how much a tiger can eat. There are now fewer than 4,000 tigers left in the wild. Spot them in Ranthambore National Park, Rajasthan, India.

## GIRAFFES

Giraffes are the tallest mammals on the planet. But it's not just their legs and necks that are long: they also have tongues that can stretch up to 50 centimetres! To see these majestic creatures in the wild, you could head to a protected area in southern Africa such as Serengeti National Park in Tanzania.

## KANGAROOS

Kangaroos can hop as far as three times their own height at speeds of 44 miles per hour. They can also swim, but are unable to jump backwards! And where would you guarantee seeing a kangaroo in the wild? Kangaroo Island, of course, which is just off the coast of Adelaide in Australia.

### WHEN YOU GROW UP

Wild animals face many different threats and it is up to us to protect them. Michael Werikhe became known as the "Rhino Man" after his fundraising walks, which were up to 1,800 miles long, helped to raise awareness about the plight of the black rhino in Africa.

Notes

# 55. FIND A POCKET OF WILDERNESS IN THE CITY

Just beyond your front door an adventure is waiting. Cities and towns are brimming with hidden nature spots, so get a local map and look for green spaces among the maze of streets. Make it your mission to find out what's in those parks, gardens and squares. Is there a clump of trees, a lake or a hidden path? Perhaps there's a flock of pigeons that gather every morning at dawn or an army of slugs that come out in the rain? You might also spot peregrine falcons, kingfishers, badgers, foxes and squirrels. In fact, you'll never know until you go and explore for yourself.

# 56. TAKE A DIFFERENT ROUTE TO SCHOOL

How many things do you do each school morning that are the same? Have breakfast, get dressed, brush your teeth, high-five the cat... How about turning one part of your daily routine into an adventure by taking a different route to school?

If you normally get driven to school, plan how you could walk there. Perhaps you could even cycle, scoot or skateboard through the streets? Maybe you could run there and take an off-road trail instead of the pavement? To get started, look at a map and mark your house and your school on it. How many different routes can you plan? Are there enough routes to take a different one every day for a whole week?

# 57. HAVE A SUNSET PICNIC

No two sunsets are the same. Some turn the sky a stormy purple as the sun wriggles out from behind a swirling mass of cloud. Others light up the horizon in reds and peachy pinks.

A hill is a great location for a sunset picnic, as is a beach, riverbank or lakeshore, where you can see the sky reflected in the water. But you could also head out into your back garden or down to the local park. Make sure you pack something fantastic to eat for dinner and warm clothes to pull on when the sun finally tucks itself away. Unless you plan on sleeping out for the night, it's also a good idea to make sure that you can get back home once it's dark!

## TOP TIP

If you want the best sunset spot, look for places with a great view to the west (see Adventure 62), as that's where the sun sets.

# 58. SLEEP UNDER THE STARS FOR SEVEN NIGHTS IN A ROW

Sleeping out in the open in a tent or a bivvy is a magical experience – even for only one night. But just like the tides of the sea, the landscapes of the sky change every night too. So set yourself a challenge to sleep out under the stars for seven nights in a row. Get six friends together and spend one night camped in each person's back garden or a nearby campsite and enjoy the changing skies above you.

# 59. SWIM BETWEEN TWO POINTS OF LAND

Imagine looking out at an island and wondering who or what might be living there. It might be somewhere that you can't get to on foot or by car, so wouldn't it be brilliant if you could just slip into your swimmers and splash over to find out?

Adventures are all about exploring the unknown and there's no reason why a patch of water should stand between you and your unanswered questions. Set yourself a challenge to swim between two points of land and find out exactly what it's like on the other side of the water.

When you do make it to the other side in your point-to-point adventure, you'll feel a huge sense of satisfaction and a swell of pride in your chest. Be sure to look back, put your hands on your hips, stand tall and say loud and proud: "I just swam across that. I am amazing!"

## WHEN YOU GROW UP

Diana Nyad was the first person to swim from Cuba to Florida, USA, without a shark cage. With a team of support kayakers who had a shark-repelling device and wearing a specially designed mask to protect her from jellyfish stings, she made the crossing on her third attempt, at the age of sixty-four. It took her nearly 53 hours.

# ADVENTURE INSPIRATION

## CHOOSE YOUR ROUTE

Look on a map to find two points of land you think it might be possible to swim between. You could swim from the seashore out to an island, from one riverbank to another or to an island in the middle of a lake. Take a good look at how far the swim would be, and make sure you've swum that distance before in a pool or on a wild swim. Knowing you can make it without getting exhausted in the middle will mean you're able to enjoy the swim and keep an eye out for any wildlife.

## DECIDE ON YOUR SUPPORT TEAM

You can't do a point-to-point swim alone, so decide who to take with you on your adventure. Someone who is a stronger swimmer than you is ideal, so that you always feel safe. Will your helper(s) swim alongside you or take along a kayak or a boat?

## GETTING BACK

Work out whether you plan to swim to the point of land and back again, or just one way. If you're getting out on the other side, you'll need your support team to take your clothes for you. They can always bring a picnic with them too. Yum!

## TIME OF YEAR

Think about what time of year would be best to take on your point-to-point challenge. Rivers, lakes and oceans tend to be warmer towards the end of the summer, so that's a perfect time to take to the water.

## SWIM IN A STRAIGHT LINE

When you're swimming between two points of land, it's easy to veer off course and end up travelling in a big wiggly line. To stay in a straight line, pick something on the land that's easy to spot, like a post, flag or building. Every time you look at the land, find this same point again and head towards it.

# 60. HIKE ON A PENINSULA

Imagine that you are walking along a clifftop with swooping seagulls and the smell of salt on the breeze. Your legs are tired from the ups and downs of the path, but you are grinning from ear to ear.

A peninsula is an area of land that sticks out from the mainland and into the sea. Look at the coast nearest to you and see if you can find one, and then look for a footpath either across or around it. Take care to stick to the path and away from the edge. Pack something exciting for lunch because a clifftop picnic looking out over the sea is the best part of this adventure. Just make sure the seagulls don't steal your sandwiches!

## AROUND THE WORLD

### WHERE TO TASTE THE SEA AIR

- Coromandel Peninsula, New Zealand
- Delmarva Peninsula, USA
- Dingle Peninsula, Ireland
- Lizard Peninsula, UK
- Teke Peninsula, Turkey

# 61. TRY FREEDIVING

It's fascinating to explore underwater by diving or snorkelling, but you can leave the equipment behind and see how deep you can go using just the breath in your lungs. Freediving is very peaceful. You swim silently through the ocean, relying on the power of your lungs and the flippers on your feet. When you resurface, it feels like you are returning from another world.

The first rule of freediving is that you must never do it alone. To get started you need to practise holding your breath underwater. A swimming pool is a good place to try this. Always make sure you're with an experienced adult, so that they can make sure you pop back up!

Gradually you'll find that you can hold your breath for longer. Once you're ready to try freediving in the ocean, find a local instructor or sign up to a freediving course. Your instructor will be able to teach you the basics and loan you a pair of flippers. Flippers increase the surface area of your feet so you can travel further in a single breath.

Before you get into the water, imagine you are already there. The more you visualize yourself freediving, the more relaxed you will be when you are swimming. It's amazing how you can trick your brain into thinking you've done something lots of times when you've actually just practised with your mind!

### WHEN YOU GROW UP
Herbert Nitsch freedived 253 metres beneath the ocean's surface (that's almost the height of the Eiffel Tower). He held his breath underwater for a world-record-breaking 9 minutes, though he suffered injuries in the process.

85

# 62. USE A COMPASS

Right now you are standing on top of a giant magnet. In fact, the magnetic field from the Earth's iron core is so strong that it extends out into space! For centuries, explorers have used this magnetic field as a way to navigate across new terrain. Like every magnet, the Earth also has a North and South Pole. This means that when you use a magnetic compass, it's always possible to find the North Pole, wherever you are in the world. And once you know where north is, it's simple to work out which direction you want to head in. That's why learning to use a compass is one of the most important navigational and survival skills there is.

The most important thing to remember is that the red magnetic needle always points north. This is because the magnet in the arrow is being drawn towards the North Pole. So, once you've got a compass (they aren't too expensive to buy from an outdoor store), gather some friends in your back garden or park. Start by learning how to take a compass bearing for a specific direction.

Imagine that you find yourself out in the wilderness and a strong gust of wind rips your map from your hands and blows it away! How will you get home? You remember (from when you did have the map) that there is a river to the north-east of where you are, and if you can just find that river and follow it downstream it will lead you to a beach and your home. This is where a compass can be all you need. Setting a bearing to show you which direction is north-east will get you back on the right track.

# ⊙ HOW TO DO IT

## PARTS OF A COMPASS

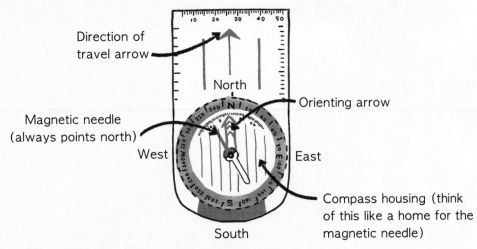

Direction of travel arrow

North

Orienting arrow

Magnetic needle (always points north)

West

East

Compass housing (think of this like a home for the magnetic needle)

South

## HOW TO TAKE A NORTH-EAST BEARING

1. Turn the compass housing so that the direction of travel arrow sits between N (north) and E (east).

2. Leave the housing alone and hold the compass flat on your palm so that the needle can move easily.

3. Turn yourself and the compass until the red magnetic needle lines up with the N (north) on the orienting arrow.

4. Now start walking in a path that lines up with the direction of travel arrow: that will take you north-east!

## COMPASS-BEARING PRACTICE

Try this exercise in your back garden or park. Set a new bearing each time you take the steps. What do you notice about where you finish up, compared with where you started?

1. Take five steps south

2. Take ten steps east

3. Take twenty steps north

4. Take fifteen steps west

5. Take fifteen steps south

6. Take five steps east

(Answer: You should end up back exactly where you started!)

# 63. LOOK AFTER AN ANIMAL

Sometimes the best friends to have an adventure with are ones with four legs. They might not speak the same language and they might do a poo right in front of you, but hanging out with animals can be just as fun as hanging out with humans. Whether you're being taught how to bottle-feed a lamb or stroking a bunny with fluffy ears, looking after animals is a rewarding experience.

 ## ADVENTURE INSPIRATION

### HORSES
Spend a day at a local stable, grooming and mucking out the horses. Horses are sensitive animals – they need love and attention to keep them happy and healthy.

### DOGS AND CATS
Volunteer at a local shelter for cats or dogs. Often the animals want to play, so you can help just by hanging out with them for a while.

### FARM ANIMALS
It'll be an early start, but you could spend the day helping on a farm. Learning how to collect eggs, feed goats and pigs, or bottle-feed lambs will give you an idea of the hard work farmers put in every day.

### PET-SIT
Offer to look after a friend's pet when they go on holiday. Maybe they have a dog that you can take for walks or perhaps they have a pet snake! You probably don't want to walk the snake, but you can learn how to care for it all the same.

# 64. TAKE ON 100 MILES OF TRAIL RUNNING

Can you imagine running 100 miles? It's a very long way, but what if you had a whole year in which to do it? It will still be a challenge, just like any good adventure should be, but it's not impossible! Think about where you can clock up those miles – perhaps it will be at school, around the local park or even in other parts of the world.

You can begin your 100-mile trail-running challenge on any day of the year you like: your birthday, next week, tomorrow even. Just mark it in the diary so that you remember for the next year.

## WHEN YOU GROW UP

Mira Rai, a professional trail runner, has raced in the Himalayas, Alps and Scottish Highlands, winning the Ben Nevis Ultra Trail Race of 75 miles in 14 hours and 24 minutes.

 HOW TO DO IT

1. Keep a record of every time you run on a trail. You could do this in a notebook or make your own wall chart.

2. Plan your challenge, so that you're not trying to cram all the miles into the last few weeks. How many miles of trail running would you need to average each week or each month?

3. Get your friends involved so that they can do their own 100-mile trail challenge. Perhaps you can run some of the miles together!

4. If you're part of a running team at school, compete in cross-country events or do a parkrun, don't forget to log those miles too.

5. Think about your reward for when you hit 100 miles. Ultimately, you'll need the motivation to come from inside, but having something extra special to reward yourself when it's done will help on the tougher days of the challenge.

# 65. CREATE YOUR OWN SCAVENGER HUNT

Scavenger hunts are epic! You get to spend the day dashing around your local neighbourhood with your friends, gathering mysterious objects and completing silly challenges. It'll be an adventure filled with surprises, twists and turns, but hunting down clues is what you do best – because you are a SCAVENGER!

To get started on your adventure, gather some friends together and split into three groups. One group can be in charge of designing and laying out the scavenger hunt, and the other two groups can be hunters, competing against each other.

If you're in the group designing the hunt, you will need to meet earlier than everyone else so that you have plenty of time to lay out the clues or come up with the hunt design.

# ADVENTURE INSPIRATION

## THE DETECTIVE HUNT

Leave clues at each location, letting the hunters know where to go next. The clues could relate to special places that only you and your friends know about.

## THE COLLECTION HUNT

List a series of items that the hunters need to find and bring back, such as pieces of litter, a certain type of leaf, a feather or a coin. The first team of hunters back at base with all the items wins a prize.

## THE ACTIVITY HUNT

This is just like a collection hunt except that you have a list of things that the hunters have to do as a group – and instead of objects, the hunters bring back photos of them doing the activities on the list. Can the whole group fit into a phone box? Or stage a dance challenge in the middle of a crowded street? Put anything that could be embarrassing or make you giggle on the list for your friends to do.

## THE MAP HUNT

Draw a map of your local area that shows items hidden in various locations. Once all the objects are collected and put together, they should form a final clue to let the hunters know where the ultimate prize is.

**TOP TIP**

Find the right balance between easy and tricky. If your hunt is too hard, you'll be there all day. If it's too easy, it won't be enough of a challenge for the hunters.

# 66. GO SCRAMBLING

Scrambling is an adventure that's partway between hiking and rock climbing. Use your hands to keep your balance as you edge slowly up and along a mountain ridge. You'll need to hold your nerve, and not think too much about the steep drop on each side!

It's exhilarating to explore a mountain's hidden nooks and crannies, where each new boulder or rock formation is its own mini-challenge. Your strength and strategic moves will be rewarded with amazing views of the mountains and valleys below.

## 🧭 HOW TO DO IT

1. Find an expert who knows the area and the best route to take.

2. Choose your footwear carefully – trainers or boots with good grip are essential.

3. When you're scrambling, look for less-steep sections of rock with ledges for your feet. Look for rocks that you can wrap your fingers around and use as handholds. Often the best routes reveal themselves as you go along.

4. Once you've finished a section, make sure you take a good look at what you just shimmied your way across, and stop to shout "WOWSERS!"

5. Remember that what goes up must come down. Save some energy and jelly beans for the scramble back home.

# 67. GO ON A LONG-DISTANCE CYCLING ADVENTURE

Imagine cycling away from home, knowing that you might not be coming back for weeks or months. You are in for a roller-coaster ride through everything the world has to offer - the good, the bad and the painful. By the end, you'll feel every hill in your legs, the dusty air in your lungs and the warmth of the sun on your face.

There's a real sense of freedom in exploring the world by bike. It's far quicker than walking, but better than travelling by car - where landscapes, people and places whizz past before you can check them out. You get to make the rules on a cycling adventure. You decide where to stop, what to eat, where to sleep and how far to travel. Pick your total distance and who you want to go with, and choose your route carefully along smaller roads with less traffic or even traffic-free cycleways.

> **WHEN YOU GROW UP**
> How about cycling 18,000 miles around the planet? Mark Beaumont has done this not once, but twice. On his second attempt, he set a new record for the fastest journey around the world by bike, completing the distance in 78 days and 14 hours, cycling an average of 230 miles per day.

# 68. CREATE AN UPCYCLED HERB GARDEN

A herb garden is an easy way to begin growing your own food. Make your garden out of upcycled objects such as old tins, plastic bottles, toy cars, wellington boots, wooden crates or even car tyres. When you've chosen your planter, paint and decorate it, then fill it with compost. Plant your herbs and keep them watered in a sunny spot until they're ready to be picked for a delicious salad or sandwich.

# 69. GO ON A CANAL BOAT JOURNEY

Canals are man-made waterways that were originally built to transport goods, but now they are mainly used for fun. A canal boat adventure mixes the best bits of being on the move with all the comforts of home (including a squishy bed to curl up in each night). You'll need to learn how to cast off, steer and operate complex locks that raise and lower the canal boat in the water. And it's handy to know how to tie a bowline knot (see Adventure 25) to moor up on the bank at the end of the day. If life on board ever gets too slow, hop off at a lock and see if you can race the boat along the towpath.

Not many people have a friend who owns a canal boat, but if you seek out your nearest canal you can find out how to hire a boat for the day or longer. And if you can't hire one, enjoy exploring the canal banks. Towpaths are perfect for walking, cycling and picnicking with your pals.

# 70. VISIT A VOLCANO

A volcanic eruption is one of the world's greatest and most dangerous natural occurrences. Pressure from gas in the Earth's core builds up and becomes so intense that it has to escape through the surface. The ground gives way and molten rock and lava launch into the air.

Most of the world's volcanoes are extinct and all that remains of their explosive past are distinctive cone-shaped mountains or craters. But there are still some active volcanoes on the planet, where you can see the Earth releasing steam, smoke rings or even oozing lava.

Before heading off on your adventure, you'll need to decide whether you want to see an active volcano (one that erupts regularly) or a dormant volcano (one that could erupt but hasn't for a while). You'll probably also want to take a parent with you, just to make sure you don't end up being sizzled like a fried egg.

## AROUND THE WORLD

### DORMANT VOLCANOES

- ⊕ Mount Ararat, Turkey
- ⊕ Mount Edziza, Canada
- ⊕ Mount Kilimanjaro, Tanzania
- ⊕ Mount Pelée, Martinique
- ⊕ Mount Rainier, USA

### ACTIVE VOLCANOES

- ⊕ Kelimutu, Indonesia
- ⊕ Kīlauea, USA
- ⊕ Katla, Iceland
- ⊕ Mount Vesuvius, Italy
- ⊕ Yellowstone Caldera, USA

# 71. BUILD A RAFT AND FLOAT IT

Boats and boards are great for adventuring, but there is nothing quite as satisfying as spending hours building your own raft and setting sail on it with your friends. Not only will you have fun trying to design and build the raft in the first place, but by the time you're done, you can sit back safe in the knowledge that no one in the world has a raft quite like yours!

Teamwork raft: wood, plastic barrels and rope

When you've finished building your raft, give it a name - it's bad luck to set sail on a boat without a name. Don't forget to add a flag to your design too. Before your maiden voyage, officially name your raft by wetting the bow. Pour some water over the front of the raft and announce its name very loudly and proudly to your family and friends.

Be prepared for your raft not to float - the first time at least! Wear clothes you don't mind getting wet and do a 30-minute tester in shallow water or close to the bank before you take your magical vessel further afield into deeper waters.

Fisherman's raft: two layers of wood and rope

Bottle raft: old, used plastic bottles and a wooden pallet

# ADVENTURE INSPIRATION

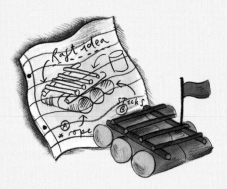

## THE BUILD

What materials will you use to build the raft? Recycled plastic barrels, bottles, wooden pallets, rope and duct tape are all raft-building essentials. Will the raft have a sail to catch the wind or be powered by you? You can find ideas online or just go for it by creating your own design. You could make a prototype of your raft first – a smaller version using the same materials – which you could test in the sink or bath.

## STEERING

How are you going to control the raft once you're out on the water? You could steer using paddles. Or if you are heading somewhere where the bottom isn't too deep, you could propel yourself along with a wooden or aluminium pole.

## THE LAUNCH LOCATION

Decide early on where you intend to sail your raft and how you will get the raft to your chosen location. Will you need to build it on the riverbank, or can you ask a parent to transport it in the car? Always start in flat, calm water.

## SAFETY

Take an adult with you and wear a buoyancy aid in case your voyage takes an exciting twist or you need rescuing somewhere along the way. It's also a good idea to check in with the local authority on the rules for being on the water. You don't want to go crashing into boats or other rival rafts and sink after spending hours making your raft float-worthy!

# 72. MAKE A SLEDGE AND TAKE IT FOR A SPIN

You are at the top of a snowy slope sitting on a sledge. You rock backwards before tipping your body weight forwards and then – *whoosh!* – you're off! As you fly down the hill, faster than you have ever gone before, you're racing your friends, determined to win.

There's no two ways about it – sledging is awesome! You can buy or borrow a sledge, but making your own and seeing if it'll survive the ride is a lot of the fun. The key to a good sledge is a smooth, flat bottom that will allow you to pick up a decent amount of speed as you slide.

## WHEN YOU GROW UP

Vonetta Flowers dreamed of becoming an Olympian. When she failed to make the track-and-field team, she turned to bobsledding. Two years later, she and her teammate made history by winning gold at the first Olympic bobsled event for women.

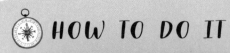 # HOW TO DO IT

YOU WILL NEED:

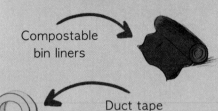

Compostable bin liners

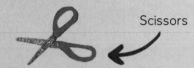 Sturdy cardboard box (packing box or takeaway pizza box)

Duct tape

Scissors

1. Flatten your cardboard box into a rectangular shape and tape it into position. You can create a lip at the back to stop your bottom getting wet.

2. Wrap the cardboard in the bin liners. Try to make the layers as smooth as possible so there's nothing to catch on the ground.

3. Tape around the edges of the cardboard to keep the bin liner in place.

4. You're good to go! Head out of the door and to your chosen hill. Local parks are good as there are fewer trees and more open space for a clear run.

## TOP TIP

If there are no hills nearby, you could always use your sledge on a flat patch of snow-covered grass. Tie a piece of rope to the front of your sledge and get a friend to pull you along the ground.

# 73. GO FAT-BIKING

With their thick and chunky tyres, fat bikes will go where other bikes can't. On a fat bike you can pedal your way along a coastline, glide down giant desert dunes or suck in fresh mountain air as you explore a wintery wonderland. Fat bikes allow you to go off-road and over all kinds of obstacles, including roots, rocks, snow, ice and sand, so you'll need a helmet to keep your head safe.

Because you'll be biking on difficult terrain, remember that you'll cover far less distance on a fat bike than you would on a normal mountain bike. It will be harder work too – but double the fun!

## WHEN YOU GROW UP
Wildlife enthusiast Ness Knight used a fat bike to explore 600 miles of desert in a remote part of Namibia. She travelled alone in up to 49°C heat and came across lions and elephants.

## ADVENTURE INSPIRATION

### SNOW FAT-BIKING
If you're going fat-biking in the snow, make sure you keep every part of your body covered and warm. Also think about how you'll carry your water. If you're heading out in sub-zero temperatures, use a Thermos or insulated bottle. There's nothing worse than gasping for a drink after an uphill climb, only to find that your water has turned to a big chunk of ice!

### SAND FAT-BIKING
If you're heading out on the sand, try to find the perfect riding spot. If you are too far inland, you'll start to sink in the soft, dry sand, but if you are too close to the sea, the wet sand will feel like quicksand. Find a line on the beach that's somewhere between the two. Don't forget to explore any sand dunes too. Push your bike to the top of a dune and carve your way down to the bottom. It might take a bit of practice, but once you get the hang of it, it'll feel like you're floating!

# 74. TRY SAND-SURFING

The ocean isn't the only place where you can surf. For an adrenaline-fuelled ride why not try sliding your way down a massive sand dune? After the thrill of the descent, you'll want to get right back to the top and do it all over again – only better, faster and with more turns.

Lots of sand-surfing dunes are easily accessed by road. Ask an adult to drive you and your friends to the nearest dune. It's also a good idea to hire a sandboard. You could try skidding down on a tea tray or ocean boogie board, but the bottom of sandboards are specially designed to allow you to pick up speed over the coarse grains of sand.

When you hire a board, you can choose between standing upright and strapping your feet in (like snowboarding) or going for the simpler option of lying on your tummy and careering down the dune head first. The tummy version is easier for beginners and you can go faster! *Yeeeeehaaaaww!*

Save some energy for the climb back up the dune. You'll need to work out how to carry your board and get into a rhythm to reach the top. Sand-surfing is tiring stuff, so an hour on the dunes will be plenty of time for an adventure.

## TOP TIP

Even though you'll be hollering with excitement as you speed down the dune, remember to keep your mouth closed as much as possible, unless you want a sand sandwich for lunch!

## AROUND THE WORLD

### SAND-SURFING SPOTS

🌐 Atlantis Dunes, South Africa

🌐 Monte Kaolino, Germany

🌐 Huacachina, Peru

🌐 Oregon Dunes, USA

🌐 Te Paki Sand Dunes, New Zealand

# 75. GO CAVING

Beneath our feet is a fascinating underworld: an adventure playground of sparkling caves, dark tunnels and underground lakes. On a caving adventure, you'll come across the most amazing, wonderful and downright weird places on Planet Earth. The only question is are you brave enough to venture down into the dark?

## AROUND THE WORLD

### WONDERS BENEATH THE SURFACE

- Eisriesenwelt, Austria
- Fingal's Cave, UK
- Krubera Cave, Georgia
- Mammoth Cave, USA
- Waitomo Glowworm Caves, New Zealand

# ADVENTURE INSPIRATION

## CHOOSE THE RIGHT CAVE

There are lots of caves around the world where you can experience the magic of the underworld without needing to wriggle through too many small, enclosed spaces.

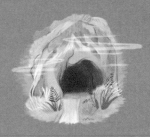

## GO WITH A PROFESSIONAL

Before you start exploring, it's essential to know that the cave is safe. Start by visiting a caving centre. There you'll have an instructor who can show you the right routes and make sure you have the necessary equipment.

## WEAR THE RIGHT CLOTHES

Choose clothes that are warm, light and close to your skin. They should also be able to withstand some wear and tear as you squeeze, scramble and crawl on your underground adventure.

## UNDERSTAND YOUR BODY

Before you enter a cave, think about your body shape and just how many different sizes and shapes you can become. Can you make yourself flat and wide, or long and thin? Knowing how to get your body into different positions will help you move in tighter spaces underground.

## REMEMBER TO BREATHE

If you ever feel stuck in a cave, change your focus so you aren't thinking about where you are or what position your body is in, but about your breathing instead. Getting your breathing under control will help you stay relaxed and you'll find a solution to the challenge you're facing.

# 76. TELL SPOOKY STORIES

Nothing delivers an adrenaline rush like a good spooky story. Do you live near a graveyard, a creepy patch of dark forest or an old haunted house? Gather your friends and an adult to supervise, and plan a visit to the creepiest place you know. Take a warm jacket, a hat, some snacks and a torch, and wait until it is dark. It's a well-known fact that ghosts, ghouls and goblins only come out to play at night.

Once you reach your chosen spot, tell your spine-chilling stories by torchlight. Now you can discover who is the bravest of you all...

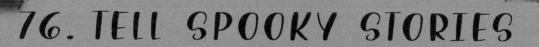

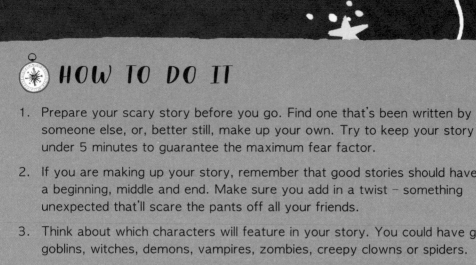

# HOW TO DO IT

1. Prepare your scary story before you go. Find one that's been written by someone else, or, better still, make up your own. Try to keep your story under 5 minutes to guarantee the maximum fear factor.

2. If you are making up your story, remember that good stories should have a beginning, middle and end. Make sure you add in a twist – something unexpected that'll scare the pants off all your friends.

3. Think about which characters will feature in your story. You could have ghosts, goblins, witches, demons, vampires, zombies, creepy clowns or spiders.

4. Don't forget gruesome or creepy details. Describe a witch's bulging warts, the feeling of hot breath on your neck and the creak of a door opening.

5. Use your voice to add to the atmosphere of the story: shout, whisper and make sound effects. And don't forget to use the power of suggestion. Where *is* that knocking sound coming from?

# 77. RIDE A UNICYCLE

Lots of people go adventuring on two wheels, but why not head out on just one? Riding a unicycle is the ultimate test of skill, balance and endurance.

It takes a lot of practice, but if you're able to master this skill, you'll be among the few people in the world who can call themselves a unicyclist.

Find out what it's like to ride a unicycle by taking a class with an instructor or teaching yourself from books and online videos. It'll take time to find your balance and build up the strength in your legs, but you'll soon be pedalling like a big-top performer and then ... the world is yours to explore.

### WHEN YOU GROW UP

Ed Pratt rode around the world on a unicycle when he was nineteen, travelling 21,000 miles through twenty-five countries over more than three years. He carried with him a tent, sleeping bag, camping stove and all the kit he needed to make the journey alone.

 ## HOW TO DO IT

1. Find a unicycle! See if there's a club in your area where you can borrow one.

2. Make sure your unicycle is the right height. There should be a slight bend in your knee when the pedal is fully pushed down.

3. Find a wall to help you balance. Avoid fences or anything you might be tempted to cling to, as these will throw your weight off-centre. Better still, find a friend and hold on to their shoulder.

4. Sit on the unicycle with your weight slightly forward or centred above the wheel. This can feel scary so try to stay relaxed. Use the wall or your friend to help you. Remember, the worst thing that's going to happen is that you will lose your balance and need to put a foot on the floor.

5. Practice makes perfect. Take it little by little, day by day and soon you'll be ready to take your unicycle on adventures further afield.

6. Once you've learned to unicycle, can you set yourself a goal to ride a mile?

# 78. DAM A STREAM

Water is one of the most powerful forces in nature, changing the shape of the landscape as it carves through rocks and rushes over plains, surging towards the sea. Water is wild, unruly and doesn't like to be told what to do. That's why building a dam and capturing the power of the water is such fun, especially on a sunny day.

Dams work best in flat and shallow streams, where the flow is gentle and you can stand up in the water without fearing you'll be swept off your feet. Top dam spots are inland streams, which feed into bigger rivers, or small streams on the beach which flow out to the sea. You should be able to spot these streams marked by faint blue lines on a map.

When you've found the perfect stream, gather a mixture of rocks, twigs, leaves and seaweed – anything natural which will stop the flow of the water. Put a friend in charge of gathering and another in charge of building, and get damming! Don't forget to break the dam when you leave.

**TOP TIP**

Mix the sizes of your dam materials. Big rocks are useful to quickly form the dam, but you need smaller stones or twigs to plug the gaps too, or the water will still find a way through.

# 79. LISTEN AND LOOK FOR BIRDS

You don't need to go far for a birdwatching adventure. You could start right this moment, by listening to what you can hear from your balcony, back garden or local park. Chances are you will be able to hear the birds before you can see them. Shut your eyes – how many different bird calls are there? One of nature's greatest wonders is the dawn chorus, when birds sing as the sun rises. So early morning is the perfect time to head outside with a notebook and bird-spotting guide or app, and identify the birds you hear and see.

# 80. CLIMB A TREE

Grab a friend and head to your local wood or park. Look for a knobbly, gnarly, thick-trunked tree (like an oak tree or a weeping willow) where the branches are low to the ground and ready to offer you a leg-up to the sky. Start climbing steadily and keep an eye out for wildlife on the way.

# 81. VISIT THE HIGHEST POINT IN YOUR AREA

There's something wonderful about being high on a hill, looking down on the land below. From the top of a hill, the world feels different and all your worries are carried away on the wind. So why not get a fresh perspective and visit the highest point in your area? You can find this by looking on a map. High points of land will be marked with a little triangle and a number (the number tells you how high the top is), or with contour lines (the thin lines that mark where hills are, see Adventure 31).

Once you've found your hill, work out the best route to the top. Does it look like there's a trail to follow, or will you have to make your own way? If there isn't a hill nearby, is there a tall building or landmark you could climb to the top of instead?

# 82. GO ON A
# SEA-KAYAKING ADVENTURE

You're crashing through the waves, riding high on the ocean. Seagulls swirl above you as you summon the energy for the final few paddle strokes that will take you to shore. Your mind is whirring with the memories of a day spent exploring the coastline, ducking in and out of sandy coves and caves... You have been on a sea-kayaking adventure!

Sea kayaking is thrilling because no two days on the sea are ever the same. Some days it might be calm, but other days you'll fight to handle it. You also never know what you might see from your kayak. This adventure is a great way to see dolphins, shoals of fish, puffins or seals up close.

## WHEN YOU GROW UP

Sarah Outen and Justine Curgenven spent 101 days kayaking over 1,500 miles along Alaska's Aleutian chain, a remote string of islands in the wild waters of the Pacific Ocean. As well as meeting plenty of farting sea lions, Sarah also encountered a grizzly bear while washing in a river!

## TOP TIP

Keep your grip on the paddle relaxed as you explore. If you hold the paddle tightly for hours on end, you'll get a cold and stiff hand.

# ADVENTURE INSPIRATION

## LEARN THE BASICS

Find a local kayaking centre and instructor who can teach you how to get in and out of the kayak, how to paddle and what to do if you capsize (the technical term for tipping upside down). It's best to learn on flat, calm water in a quiet bay, before progressing to full expeditions on wilder high seas. You'll always need to wear a buoyancy aid too.

## PERFECT YOUR TECHNIQUE

Sit up straight in the kayak, with your knees slightly bent. Kayak paddles have two blades. Hold the shaft of the paddle a little wider than your shoulders. Place one blade in the water and pull it towards you. Then do the same on the other side of the boat and you should go in a straight line.

## GET A GUIDE FOR WILDLIFE-WATCHING

Once you're comfortable and confident in your kayak on calm water, you'll want to progress to guided trips further afield. A guide will know all the best scenic routes and wildlife-watching spots along the coast.

## CAMP OVERNIGHT

Start with day trips and then move on to journeys which include an overnight camp. There's nothing better than paddling all day long on the sea, then pulling into a deserted sandy beach and lighting a campfire to spend a night sleeping under the stars.

# 83. TRY BOULDERING

Bouldering is the ultimate brain-and-body puzzle. Using just your hands and feet, with no ropes, you have to find the best route across a rock face. Each and every move will test both your mind and fitness.

There are many places where you can go bouldering, such as gyms, city parks or even national parks. The golden rule is you should never be more than 6 metres from the ground. Climbing shoes, with flexible soles, will help you grip every tiny hold. Whether you are indoors or outdoors, have a crash mat in place to catch you and make sure you've always got someone to stand beside the mat and spot you when you fall.

## TOP TIP

Work on your finger strength. Train them just as you would any other part of your body and you'll find that you can cling on to small holds and find new routes up the rock face.

## HOW TO DO IT

1.  In bouldering, you use your legs more than your arms. As a beginner, it's natural to want to use your upper body to pull yourself up. But given that your leg muscles are much bigger and stronger, try to pick routes that allow you to push off from your legs. Just use your hands for support.

2.  Keep your hips close to the wall as you climb. This will give you more flexibility and stop your centre of gravity getting too low.

3.  Remember that three is a magic number! Always try to have three points of contact with the wall: ideally two feet and one hand, but, if needs be, as you are moving, two hands and one foot. Once you get down to just two points of contact, a fall is usually not far away!

4.  Place your feet and hands gently and deliberately on the wall. This will encourage you to slow down and think more carefully about your chosen route.

5.  Don't be afraid of falling onto the mat! Falling off, trying new moves and testing yourself is all part of the fun. Be patient and have confidence that you'll improve gradually.

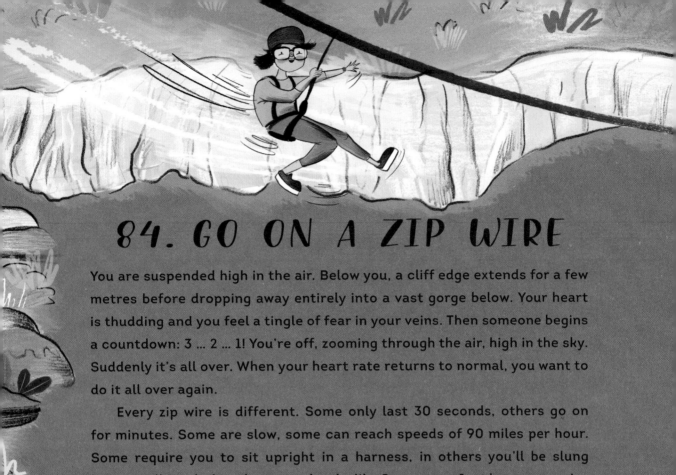

# 84. GO ON A ZIP WIRE

You are suspended high in the air. Below you, a cliff edge extends for a few metres before dropping away entirely into a vast gorge below. Your heart is thudding and you feel a tingle of fear in your veins. Then someone begins a countdown: 3 ... 2 ... 1! You're off, zooming through the air, high in the sky. Suddenly it's all over. When your heart rate returns to normal, you want to do it all over again.

Every zip wire is different. Some only last 30 seconds, others go on for minutes. Some are slow, some can reach speeds of 90 miles per hour. Some require you to sit upright in a harness, in others you'll be slung horizontally and whoosh across the sky !ike Superman. Just because you've tried one zip wire, it doesn't mean that the next one won't surprise you!

## AROUND THE WORLD

### WHERE TO TEST YOUR NERVE

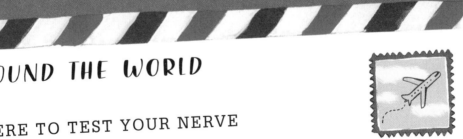

- 🌐 Fly Toledo, Spain
- 🌐 Jebel Jais Flight, United Arab Emirates
- 🌐 Louisville Mega Cavern, USA
- 🌐 Toro Verde Adventure Park, Puerto Rico
- 🌐 Zip World, Bethesda, UK

# 85. EXPLORE ROCK POOLS

Millions of exciting creatures make their homes beneath the ocean's waves. You can sneak a peek at ocean life without having to stray from the shore by exploring the small pockets of marine wonder in rock pools.

You'll find all kinds of things in a rock pool - a starfish, a spiky sea urchin, a dancing anemone, or perhaps an orange-beaked oystercatcher on the hunt for its next meal. Each rock pool is a new world teeming with tiny, yet incredible, forms of life.

👀 SPOTTER'S GUIDE: ROCK POOLS

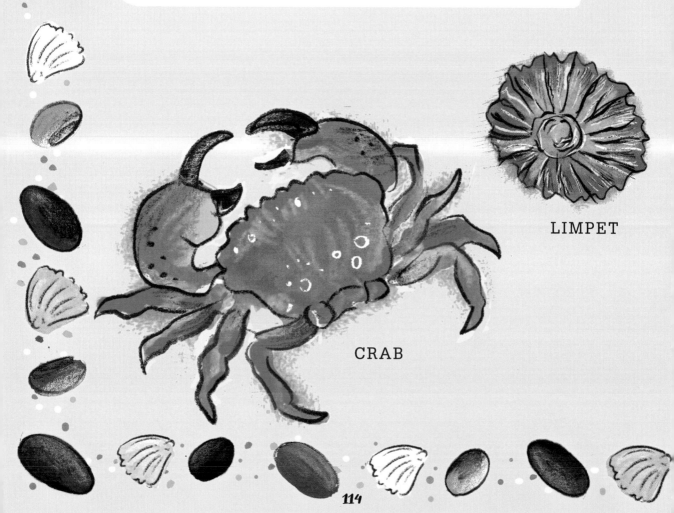

CRAB

LIMPET

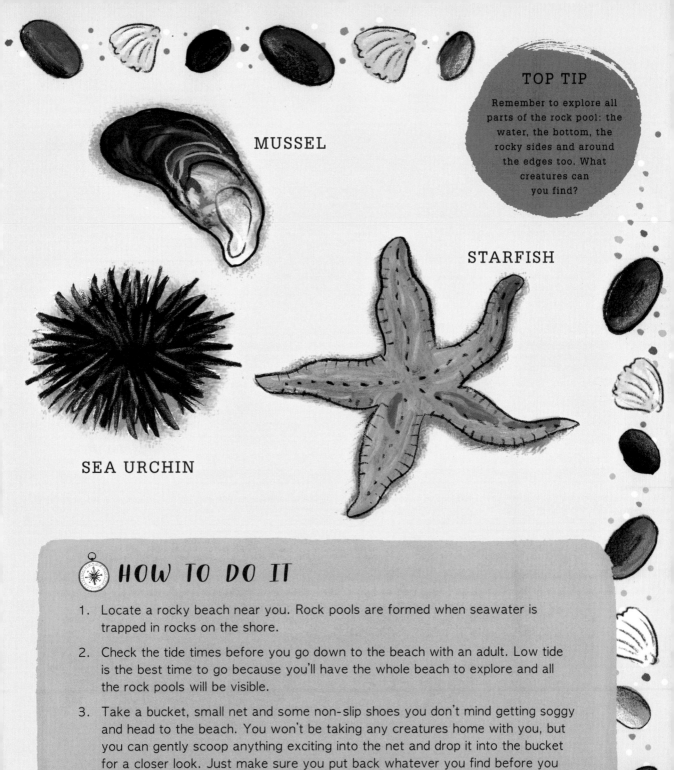

MUSSEL

**TOP TIP**

Remember to explore all parts of the rock pool: the water, the bottom, the rocky sides and around the edges too. What creatures can you find?

STARFISH

SEA URCHIN

## ⊕ HOW TO DO IT

1. Locate a rocky beach near you. Rock pools are formed when seawater is trapped in rocks on the shore.

2. Check the tide times before you go down to the beach with an adult. Low tide is the best time to go because you'll have the whole beach to explore and all the rock pools will be visible.

3. Take a bucket, small net and some non-slip shoes you don't mind getting soggy and head to the beach. You won't be taking any creatures home with you, but you can gently scoop anything exciting into the net and drop it into the bucket for a closer look. Just make sure you put back whatever you find before you leave. You wouldn't like it if someone took you away from your home!

# 86. DRINK FROM A NATURAL SPRING

Have you noticed that water has a different taste depending on where you are in the world? The tap water you drink each day has gone through a treatment and filtration process to remove any nasty bits. But if you visit a natural spring, you can trust nature to have done the filtering and drink ice-cold water that tastes fresh and delicious.

Natural springs are normally high in the mountains and get their water from glaciers or melted snow. This means the water is fresh from the ground and hasn't had time to run over the land and collect dirt like sheep poop! Spring water is clear and ready to drink. It's so ready to drink, in fact, that water companies bottle water from springs and then sell it.

But you don't need to pay a penny for spring water! Often towns close to a spring's source have a drinking fountain, or you can find a natural spring in the countryside. Many people will record where they've found a spring, so if you know the location, you can head out on a hike and enjoy a refreshing drink when you get there.

## AROUND THE WORLD

### WHERE TO SAMPLE A NATURAL SPRING

- 🌐 Big Red Spring, USA
- 🌐 Évian-les-Bains, France
- 🌐 Loch Sheanta, UK
- 🌐 Shasui Falls, Japan
- 🌐 Te Waikoropupū Springs, New Zealand

# 87. GO ABSEILING

The first time you try abseiling, you will probably feel a bit nervous. It goes against every survival instinct to lower yourself on a rope down a steep drop. But once you get a taste of the adrenaline that comes from stepping off that ledge, you'll feel like such a superhero that you'll want another go.

Abseiling is an exhilarating way to explore outdoors. You can do it down moss-covered waterfalls, ancient cliffs and even down the side of tall buildings. Every abseil is different and each one brings its own challenges.

To get started on your abseil adventure, you'll need to find an expert to teach you. You can do this through a local outdoors centre or even at an indoor climbing wall – both of these are great places to learn the basics. The instructor will be able to provide all of the ropes, a safety harness and a helmet. You'll begin by slowly walking down the wall or cliff. Be patient and build your skills and confidence slowly. Trust the rope and your instructor. It might not feel like it, but the rope will take your weight, as long as you sit down into it and then tiptoe downwards. Learn to enjoy the initial feeling of fear and the continual nervous fizz in your tummy as you move on to harder and harder descents.

**WHEN YOU GROW UP**

"Daring Doris" Long, a great-great-grandma, took up abseiling when she was 85 and went on to abseil 100 metres down a building, at 101 years of age! She holds the record for the world's oldest abseiler.

# 88. LEARN TO ROLLERBLADE

It's time to get your feet ready to rock ... and roll! Rollerblading means you can explore at a pace that's faster than walking but slower than cycling, and certainly more of a challenge than both! Rollerblading will improve your balance and leave you with legs that are strong enough for any adventure.

# 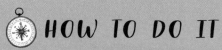 HOW TO DO IT

1. Find a pair of rollerblades that fit. There should be space for you to wiggle your toes, but each boot should be snug enough to stop your foot moving around inside. Perhaps you've got a friend who wouldn't mind lending you a pair, or a local park where you can hire some. And if you decide you like rollerblading, save up for your own pair!

2. Get used to your blades by walking on a patch of grass or carpet. These surfaces will grip the wheels and help you find your balance in the boots. And if you do fall over, you'll have a soft landing!

3. When it comes to moving on a tarmac surface, roll one foot forwards at a diagonal angle and use your back leg to push off. Then move the back leg out diagonally and roll forwards on that one. Push lightly from foot to foot at first, until you get your confidence up.

4. Keep your knees slightly bent when you skate. Having bent legs will give you more flexibility.

5. Glide like a swan on water. A swan moves smoothly because its legs are taking long, smooth strokes underneath the surface. Your legs should do that too. Once you push off one leg, take the time to let your speed slow before switching to the other foot. When you start learning, there'll be a tendency to waddle like a penguin, stepping quickly from one foot to the other to keep your balance! Be less penguin and more swan.

6. Keep protected. You will fall over so wear wrist guards, knee pads and a helmet.

7. Practise stopping. It's all very well learning how to go forwards, but knowing how to stop will prevent you from crashing into walls, bumping into kerbs or hugging passers-by. Bring your wheels to a halt using the brake at the back of the boot.

8. Be patient. Have confidence that even if rollerblading is difficult at first, you'll get there, one roll at a time.

# 89. GO ON A JOURNEY BY SCOOTER

Scooters are awesome! They're faster than walking or running and way more fun. One big leg push and – *whoosh!* – you've zoomed down the road with hardly any effort at all. Scooters are also perfect for adventuring because they're small and portable, which means that you can do a little bit of scooting, then hop on a ferry or train to your next scooting spot without too much trouble at all.

Smaller scooters (often called micro scooters) are great for scooting short distances, such as to school or the shops, but if you'd like to go adventuring somewhere new then you need to upgrade to MEGA WHEELS! The bigger the wheels on your scooter, the further you'll go with each leg push.

## WHEN YOU GROW UP
Nicolai Bangsgaard put his scooter to the test when he explored the Caribbean on it. He found that it was the perfect way to hop between islands, and over 45 days he travelled 600 miles through ten Caribbean countries.

##  HOW TO DO IT

1. Get some friends together and make a plan. Perhaps you could start by scooting between one another's houses, collecting your scoot-recruits one by one as you whizz around the neighbourhood. From there, you could scoot to a local landmark or your favourite park.

2. Whatever your route, make sure it is flat. Scooters don't go uphill very easily, although going downhill on them is fun! And don't forget your helmet.

3. Remember to keep switching the leg you use to push with. While it's tempting to push most of the time with your dominant (and usually stronger) leg, you could end up with one very tired and muscly limb. Better to keep it even and use both of them in turn.

# 90. RIDE A TANDEM BICYCLE

If you fancy going faster and further than you could on a bicycle, then a tandem is the perfect way to travel. There's also the added bonus that you can chat to your adventure partner really easily, because you're always right next to each other.

There are two distinct riding positions on a tandem bicycle. The person at the front is called the captain, and they're in charge of steering, changing gears and braking. They are usually the stronger rider. The person at the back is called the stoker and their job is to keep pedalling in time to power the tandem along.

If you're new to riding a tandem, then you'll likely take on the stoker position. It might feel odd to be with another person on a bike for the first few times, but remember to relax and go with the flow. Let the captain do their job, and make sure you do yours by staying in time, putting in some effort and enjoying the scenery!

Start off on a long straight bike path or stretch of quiet road to make sure you're in a comfortable riding position. Pushing off on a tandem, especially to begin with, is the most difficult thing to master. As a stoker, you'll get on the bike first, and sit with your feet on both pedals, ready to start pedalling the moment the captain signals that it's time to ... GO! Your adventure has begun!

## WHEN YOU GROW UP

Best friends and adventurers George Agate and John Whybrow spent nine months cycling 18,000 miles through thirty countries on a tandem bicycle. That's a lot of hours spent chatting!

# 91. GO SURFING

You are lying on a surfboard in the sea. You can feel the warmth of the sun on your back and the water is a sparkling blue. A wave rolls by every now and then, but you are patient, waiting for something special. Then you spot it: the perfect wave.

You turn towards the shore and paddle as hard as you can, arms pumping, mind racing, as you see if you can catch the wave... You feel a surge of power beneath the board and pop up to a standing position. Carving and swooshing, you are at one with the ocean! Then you hear a thunderous roar as the wave starts to break behind you, and the ride is over. Exhausted but pumped full of adrenaline, you turn the board around to face the horizon, and paddle out to do it all over again.

Surfing is an adventure of thrills and spills on an ocean rollercoaster. You will soon be addicted to catching waves, but always remember the golden rule of surfing: the best surfer is the one having the most fun!

# HOW TO DO IT

1. Head to a beach with a surf school. There you'll be able to take lessons with an instructor. Start on a longer board with a soft top, as it will be easier to find your balance and will hurt less when you fall off.

2. Learn to pop up, which is when you go from lying on your surfboard on your tummy to standing up on the board. You need upper-body strength to help you spring up and lunge at the same time. It helps to practise this on the beach first.

3. Get your paddling up to scratch. Being able to paddle at speed when lying on your tummy is how you catch that awesome wave.

4. Try, try and try again. Don't worry if you can't pop up on the first few, or even the first fifty attempts. Your body and your brain are still learning valuable lessons with every try.

5. Once you're up on your feet, keep your stance wide. It'll help you stay stable.

6. Leave the beach on a high! If you get slammed by a wave (it happens to everyone) don't let that be your last wave for the day. Even if it feels a bit scary, get back out there and catch a final good one before you go home.

### WHEN YOU GROW UP
Tom Butler caught and rode a massive 30-metre-high wave in Portugal that is believed to be the world's biggest wave ever surfed. With a mass of tumbling water crashing behind him, riding it, he said, was like "running away from a raging bull"!

# 92. GO ON A MULTI-DAY CANOEING ADVENTURE

Travelling by Canadian or "traditional" canoe is a great way to go exploring because it's easy to carry your supplies. Canoeing is most fun in pairs, so a journey down a river or around a lake will be a great trip with family, where you can chat and splash one another all day long.

It's a good idea to take someone who is experienced in the outdoors along on this adventure, because part of the joy of canoeing is that you can get to some really remote places. Having someone with you who knows how to pitch a tent, build a fire and even catch fish for dinner is a massive bonus (and, of course, you'll be able to help with all of those things too).

To plan your multi-day canoeing trip, you'll need to know how far you can comfortably travel in a day. You can find this out on a few tester day trips. Depending on the conditions, you should be able to cover between 10 and 15 miles per day, but remember you need to leave some energy for campfire songs and marshmallow-toasting in the evenings too.

The best places to travel long distances by canoe are gentle rivers and calm lakes. Canoes don't do well in rough conditions because they have open tops and take on water easily. Pack your kit in dry bags and store them low in the canoe to keep it stable. Remember that it's OK to let the current take you every now and then. If you're on a stretch of river where there is a bit of flow and you have someone else in the boat who's able to steer, then kick back, relax, take a rest for 10 minutes and eat some snacks. You'll feel re-energized when you pick the paddle back up.

Don't forget your buoyancy aid and a bailing bucket! These are essential, should you run into rough water. The bailing bucket is used to empty out the boat and stop it from sinking, and the buoyancy aid will help you float if you do capsize.

## TOP TIP

If you have to duck to avoid a low-hanging obstacle, make sure you lean forwards and not sideways. If you move sideways suddenly, you will capsize!

# AROUND THE WORLD

## AMAZING CANOEING DESTINATIONS

- 🌍 Bowron Lake Provincal Park, Canada
- 🌍 Danube River, Europe
- 🌍 Everglades National Park, USA
- 🌍 Mackenzie River, Canada
- 🌍 Sai River, Japan

### WHEN YOU GROW UP

Emma Wiggs holds a "Grand Slam" in paracanoeing, as a World, European and Paralympic champion. When training, she eats up to twenty-five eggs a week!

# 93. BUILD A SNOW CAVE AND SLEEP IN IT

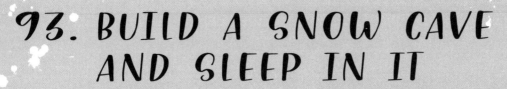

Knowing how to build a snow cave is a useful survival skill. This is one adventure where you'll definitely need an expert to show you how it's done. You should never build a snow cave alone because it might end up collapsing on you. Try asking at your local outdoor centre or Guides or Scouts group. Once you've found an expert, grab your shovel, plenty of warm layers and your sleeping gear, then head out with them into the snow!

It'll take you between 3 and 5 hours to build your snow cave, so be prepared for that before you begin. Remember that you want the cave to shelter you from the wind as much as possible.

# HOW TO DO IT

1. Look for snow that is around 1.5 metres deep. If the snow isn't that deep naturally, you can pile it up from the surrounding area. Ideally a snow cave should sleep just two people. The smaller the shelter, the more stable the roof and walls are.

2. You need air vents in your snow cave to allow oxygen in, so put two sticks into the snow. When you've finished the build, pull them out to create the vents.

3. Dig a tunnel the length of your body in the snow. Keep pushing the snow out behind you. If you've got enough snow, try to angle this tunnel slightly upwards. Hot air rises so this will mean that your snow cave is warmer.

4. At the end of the tunnel, make a T-shape. This will create two sleeping compartments, one either side of the main tunnel. Always make sure there is one person outside the cave when you're digging inside it.

5. Then dig out a dome above your head. Do this gradually. You're aiming to make sure that the walls of your snow cave are at least 30 centimetres thick, both for stability and warmth. Don't get carried away and dig so much out that you burst through the snow!

6. Once your cave is complete, use some of the snow you've dug out to block the entrance. This will allow the temperature in the cave to rise, and you should hit a toasty warm 0°C!

7. Remember that there is always a chance that your snow cave might collapse. Keep your safety in mind: always have an adult with you, and mark the outside of your snow cave clearly with small poles and fluorescent ties so people can see that a shelter has been built there. Also sleep with a shovel at your side – just in case of a collapse or a storm and you need to dig yourself out.

### WHEN YOU GROW UP

Barbara Hillary knows how to survive the snow. She reached the North Pole at the age of seventy-five and the South Pole at the age of seventy-nine, becoming the first recorded African-American woman to reach both poles.

# 94. GO GEOCACHING

Geocaching is a bit like a giant, worldwide treasure hunt. The name comes from "geo", which means Earth, and "cache", which means a hidden storage place for valuable items. The aim of this adventure is to seek out caches that have been left by other people in secret places.

Your search will lead you to unexplored pockets of your hometown, or to beautiful places further afield. It's exciting to discover somewhere off the beaten track. So what are you waiting for? Get some friends together and head out to find geocaches hidden near your home!

 ## HOW TO DO IT

1. Use an online geocache website or download an app to look up where there might be geocaches hidden near you.

2. Choose a cache and take down the coordinates of where to find it. (Coordinates are a pair of numbers that will help you to locate any place on Earth.)

3. Use a map or the geocache app to find your way to the hidden cache.

4. Once you find the geocache location, start hunting around for the hidden item. The website or app will have a detailed description of what you're looking for: some are more hidden than others!

5. Inside the cache will be a logbook and some small trinkets.

6. Sign the logbook. You can take something from the cache if you leave something else of equal value in its place.

# 95. VISIT A LIGHTHOUSE

Lighthouses are the coolest buildings on the planet! No two lighthouses are the same, but they are normally built on rugged coastlines to guide ships away from rocks. A journey to a lighthouse is also a journey back through time. Visit one to learn about the pirates and smugglers who tried to sneak ashore. You'll also catch a glimpse of the jagged rocks that caused shipwrecks in years gone by. If you're visiting a working lighthouse, you might be able to go inside to meet a lighthouse keeper and see the gigantic lamp that shines out to sea. Double adventure whammy!

## AROUND THE WORLD

### LIGHTHOUSES TO EXPLORE

- Cape Hatteras Lighthouse, USA
- Cape Reinga Lighthouse, New Zealand
- Faro de Conchupata, Bolivia
- Hook Lighthouse, Ireland
- La Vieille, France

# 96. TRACK WILD ANIMALS

Tracking wild animals is about the thrill of the unknown: you never know what you'll find. Chances are that you will spy something if you look carefully, because we share this planet with well over a million different species of animal.

Choose a trail that passes through woodland, runs alongside a river or along the beach. There are two ways to track wildlife: poop and prints! Look carefully at the ground as you walk. Muddy or snowy trails are great places for tracking, because prints tend to be more visible. Take a sketchbook or camera with you to record your findings and then look them up when you get home. If you're lucky enough to spot the animal, be sure to quietly watch what it's up to and not disturb it.

 SPOTTER'S GUIDE: PRINTS AND POOP

OWL

DEER

SNAKE

ELEPHANT

BEAR

HEDGEHOG

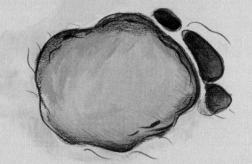

# 97. PITCH A TENT

There is nothing better than spending a night camped out with friends: warming yourself around a campfire and toasting marshmallows, then snuggling into a cosy sleeping bag. But unless you're sleeping in a den or bivvy bag (see Adventures 5 and 17), you'll need to learn how to pitch a tent.

Each tent is pitched differently. On one hand this is great, because you'll never get bored of learning, but on the other, it means you can never relax and think that tent-pitching is easy. Here are some general tips and tricks that'll help you pitch your own pop-up adventure palace, time and time again.

## TOP TIP

If your tent has separate inner and outer layers that clip together, leave the inner layer attached when you take the tent down. This will save you having to reattach it next time.

# ADVENTURE INSPIRATION

## HAVE A TEST RUN

Test out pitching your tent in your back garden or local park first. That way you'll get familiar with what bits go where. This is especially helpful if you end up arriving at your camping spot in the dark and have to pitch by torchlight.

## CHECK YOUR KIT

Before you leave your house on your adventure, check that you have all the poles and tent pegs. There's nothing worse than making it to a lovely campsite and realizing you've left the poles and pegs at home. *Doh!*

## CHOOSE YOUR PITCH WISELY

You won't want to sleep on a bumpy patch of ground, and pitching on a slope could lead to you waking up in a crumpled heap at one end of the tent!

## WORK TOGETHER

Four hands are better than two when it comes to tent-pitching. Get the corners in place first. Once the corners are pegged down, putting the rest of the tent up becomes easier.

## AIR YOUR TENT

When you get the tent home, don't leave it in the bag. Unpack it and let it air before you pack it away again. You don't want to pitch it a few months later to find it smells like wet dog. *Ewwww!*

# 98. GO ON A LONG-DISTANCE HIKE

Walking is a simple way to travel. You don't need much equipment: there's just you, your feet, a backpack and whoever you choose to take with you on your adventure. All you need is to take that first step.

A long-distance hike is the perfect adventure to go on with friends, especially if you're going to be camping each night. When you're weary after a long day of walking, having a group to share campfire stories with as you toast marshmallows is a major bonus.

## WHEN YOU GROW UP
A hike is as long as you want it to be. Mario Rigby walked across the entire continent of Africa. He covered nearly 7,500 miles, beginning his walk in South Africa and finishing in Egypt.

## AROUND THE WORLD

### EPIC HIKING TRAILS

- GR 10, France: 538 miles
- South West Coast Path, UK: 630 miles
- Great Divide Trail, Canada: 702 miles
- Tōkai Nature Trail, Japan: 1,054 miles
- Te Araroa, New Zealand: 1,900 miles

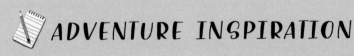

# ADVENTURE INSPIRATION

## CHOOSE YOUR ROUTE

Do some research and see if you can find a local or national trail that's over 50 miles long. If it's a designated hiking trail, there will usually be maps you can download and then signposts along the way, so you don't have to keep checking the route. Remember: you can just do part of the route – it doesn't have to be the full distance.

## DECIDE ON YOUR DAILY DISTANCE

Decide how far you can hike in a day. Take into account the fact that you'll be carrying all your gear on your back. Somewhere between 5 and 10 miles is a good aim for a day, but chat to your friends about their fitness levels and decide on a daily mileage that you're all happy with. You want to be suitably exhausted at the end of each day (it's a challenge after all) without dreading the start of the walk each morning. If you find it tough at any point, focus on the next mile rather than thinking about the whole distance.

## TAKE THE RIGHT KIT

If you're in any doubt about what shoe size to go for in hiking boots or trainers, always opt for shoes just a little bit bigger than your normal size. This will allow your toes some wiggle room, and also your feet to swell a bit when you've been on them all day.

## PACK TREATS

Whether it's your favourite chocolate bar or a bit of tomato sauce for your dinner, you will appreciate having something tasty to look forward to at the end of a long day's hike.

# 99. HOST AN OUTDOOR CINEMA NIGHT

There are four things needed to make a great movie night: good company, great snacks, an awesome film and a comfy setting to enjoy it all. So how about taking the setting to the next level and putting a twist on a movie night with your friends by creating your very own pop-up outdoor cinema!

**TOP TIP**

Check the weather forecast a few days before. You want a warm and dry evening – no one likes soggy popcorn!

 # HOW TO DO IT

## YOU WILL NEED:

Large bedsheet

Portable projector

Washing line

Clothes pegs

Bluetooth speakers

Movie (stored on a USB stick, DVD or laptop)

Pillows, blankets and a groundsheet

1. Decide who to invite to your outdoor cinema. Invite as many friends as you like. It's a good idea to have some adults around to help with the technical set-up.

2. Choose your location and a time to meet. It could be a local park, a friend's house or your back garden. If you're heading to a wild space, just make sure not to damage any trees, and to take back anything you bring with you. It will be easier to see the screen if it is dusk.

3. At your location use an existing washing line or string one up between two trees or buildings. Use the clothes pegs to hold the white bedsheet across the line. Try to get the sheet as flat as possible with no wrinkles.

4. Lay out your groundsheet, blankets and pillows. Do whatever you need to make sure you and your friends are warm and comfortable for the whole film.

5. Place the projector on the ground. Turn it on, pop in your USB stick or connect your laptop, load the movie and wiggle the projector into position. Connect your Bluetooth speakers for surround sound and hit PLAY.

# 100. GO PACKRAFTING

Packrafting is two adventures rolled into one: hiking and rafting. A packraft is an inflatable raft that packs down small enough to fit into a rucksack. With a packraft you set off on foot until you discover a patch of water that takes your fancy. Then you inflate your raft and off you go!

Packrafting allows you to explore remote lakes and rivers in rugged pockets of the world. You can slip and slide your way between rocks, paddle like crazy down raging rapids or glide effortlessly across the still waters of a lake.

Consider doing an overnight trip to try out all your gear before you head off on a longer journey. Build your confidence by starting in warm weather on smaller rivers or lakes before progressing to choppy waters and more challenging, remote landscapes.

Always adventure on the side of caution. If a river looks too scary to paddle, hike along it instead. That's the beauty of a packraft: you always have the choice.

## WHEN YOU GROW UP

Alastair Humphreys crossed a whole country by hiking and packrafting. He and a friend made a 25-day journey across Iceland, trekking across volcanic landscapes and glaciers before rafting down icy rivers.

# ADVENTURE INSPIRATION

## TAKE A COMPANION

Solo adventures are great, but as packrafting will take you to remote places with ever-changing river speeds and landscapes, you don't want to be caught out on your own. Find an adult guide who has been through the area before and can teach you what to do.

## PLAN CAREFULLY

Decide how far you want to hike and how far you want to paddle. Are you looking for a fifty–fifty split, or more paddling than walking? Work out how long it will take to cover the terrain, and therefore how much food and water you need to carry for the trip.

## PACK LIGHT

You'll need to be savvy about what goes in your pack. Remember that your packraft will weigh at least 2 kilograms on your back, so pack light. Take clothes that are going to be good for both hiking and paddling – and your buoyancy aid of course.

## KEEP YOUR KIT DRY

You are likely to get wet, but that doesn't mean your belongings should. Put everything in special dry bags and think about how to secure your kit to your raft when the water gets choppy. You don't want to end up with a soggy supper or your clothing floating somewhere upstream.

# 100 ADVENTURES CHECKLIST

Once you've completed an adventure, tick it off the list.

- ☐ CLIMB A MOUNTAIN
- ☐ BE A WASTE WARRIOR
- ☐ VISIT THE OLDEST BUILDING NEARBY
- ☐ TRAVEL BY SKI
- ☐ BUILD A DEN AND SLEEP IN IT
- ☐ GO FORAGING
- ☐ FIND A NATURAL HOT SPRING AND BATHE IN IT
- ☐ DO A FANCY-DRESS RUN
- ☐ SPEND THE NIGHT IN A WILDERNESS HUT
- ☐ GO ON A SKATEBOARDING JOURNEY
- ☐ LEARN TO WINDSURF
- ☐ LEARN TO KITESURF
- ☐ VISIT A NATURAL WONDER OF THE WORLD
- ☐ SLEEP IN A CAVE
- ☐ GO GORGE-WALKING
- ☐ CYCLE BETWEEN TWO PLACES WITH THE SAME LETTER
- ☐ BIVVY OUT IN THE WILD
- ☐ GO FOSSIL-HUNTING
- ☐ TAKE A SLEEPER TRAIN
- ☐ LEARN TO ROW
- ☐ GO ON A FLIP-A-COIN ADVENTURE
- ☐ LEARN TO SLACKLINE
- ☐ GO CLIMBING
- ☐ JOURNEY TO WHERE YOUR GRANDPARENTS WERE BORN
- ☐ TIE A BOWLINE KNOT
- ☐ TAKE A PHOTO EVERY DAY FOR A YEAR

- ☐ LEARN THE NAMES OF FOUR TREES
- ☐ GO ON A MULTI-DAY RUNNING JOURNEY
- ☐ TRACE A RIVER FROM SOURCE TO SEA
- ☐ TRAVEL TO WHERE YOUR FOOD COMES FROM
- ☐ READ A MAP
- ☐ WRITE YOUR NAME BY WALKING THE STREETS
- ☐ GO ON A TRAIL RUN
- ☐ HIKE THE SAME TRAIL IN FOUR SEASONS
- ☐ GO WILD SWIMMING
- ☐ HAVE A SEAWEED SUPPER
- ☐ RIDE A HORSE
- ☐ GO ON A NIGHT-TIME HIKE
- ☐ GO STARGAZING
- ☐ FLOAT DOWN A RIVER
- ☐ CATCH AND COOK YOUR DINNER
- ☐ GO SNORKELLING
- ☐ BUILD A TREE PLATFORM
- ☐ GO SAILING
- ☐ HIKE UP A HILL FOR A SUNRISE BREAKFAST
- ☐ GO ISLAND-HOPPING
- ☐ GO BAREFOOT WANDERING
- ☐ LEAVE A TRAIL OF KINDNESS
- ☐ LEARN TO STAND-UP PADDLEBOARD
- ☐ CYCLE UP A MOUNTAIN
- ☐ LEARN TO COUNT TO TWENTY IN THREE DIFFERENT LANGUAGES
- ☐ PUT YOUR FINGER ON A MAP AND GO!

- [ ] SLEEP IN A HAMMOCK
- [ ] SEE YOUR FAVOURITE ANIMAL IN THE WILD
- [ ] FIND A POCKET OF WILDERNESS IN THE CITY
- [ ] TAKE A DIFFERENT ROUTE TO SCHOOL
- [ ] HAVE A SUNSET PICNIC
- [ ] SLEEP UNDER THE STARS FOR SEVEN NIGHTS IN A ROW
- [ ] SWIM BETWEEN TWO POINTS OF LAND
- [ ] HIKE ON A PENINSULA
- [ ] TRY FREEDIVING
- [ ] USE A COMPASS
- [ ] LOOK AFTER AN ANIMAL
- [ ] TAKE ON 100 MILES OF TRAIL RUNNING
- [ ] CREATE YOUR OWN SCAVENGER HUNT
- [ ] GO SCRAMBLING
- [ ] GO ON A LONG-DISTANCE CYCLING ADVENTURE
- [ ] CREATE AN UPCYCLED HERB GARDEN
- [ ] GO ON A CANAL BOAT JOURNEY
- [ ] VISIT A VOLCANO
- [ ] BUILD A RAFT AND FLOAT IT
- [ ] MAKE A SLEDGE AND TAKE IT FOR A SPIN
- [ ] GO FAT-BIKING
- [ ] TRY SAND-SURFING
- [ ] GO CAVING
- [ ] TELL SPOOKY STORIES
- [ ] RIDE A UNICYCLE
- [ ] DAM A STREAM

- [ ] LISTEN AND LOOK FOR BIRDS
- [ ] CLIMB A TREE
- [ ] VISIT THE HIGHEST POINT IN YOUR AREA
- [ ] GO ON A SEA-KAYAKING ADVENTURE
- [ ] TRY BOULDERING
- [ ] GO ON A ZIP WIRE
- [ ] EXPLORE ROCK POOLS
- [ ] DRINK FROM A NATURAL SPRING
- [ ] GO ABSEILING
- [ ] LEARN TO ROLLERBLADE
- [ ] GO ON A JOURNEY BY SCOOTER
- [ ] RIDE A TANDEM BICYCLE
- [ ] GO SURFING
- [ ] GO ON A MULTI-DAY CANOEING ADVENTURE
- [ ] BUILD A SNOW CAVE AND SLEEP IN IT
- [ ] GO GEOCACHING
- [ ] VISIT A LIGHTHOUSE
- [ ] TRACK WILD ANIMALS
- [ ] PITCH A TENT
- [ ] GO ON A LONG-DISTANCE HIKE
- [ ] HOST AN OUTDOOR CINEMA NIGHT
- [ ] GO PACKRAFTING

**WARNING**
Adult supervision required for adventures.